The Animal Days

Keila Vall de la Ville

The Animal Days
First Edition 2021

© Keila Vall de la Ville

© Translation by Robin Myers

© Cover and interior illustrations: Gabriella di Stefano

© Published by katakana editores 2021 All rights reserved

Editor: Omar Villasana
Design: Elisa Orozco

ISBN: 978-1-7365650-2-5

KATAKANA EDITORES CORP.
Weston FL 33331
katakanaeditores@gmail.com

KEILA VALL DE LA VILLE

translated by Robin Myers

The Animal Days

katakana
editores

I was, in turn, and without any one hindering the others,
a saint, a traveler, a tightrope walker.

RAFAEL CADENAS

I'm going to kill my animal

rise up grown

PATRICIA GUZMÁN

Chapter I

Rafael stands on the edge of a big stone wall, waving his arms up and down like a bird, flexing his knees and flapping as if he were about to take off in flight, as if he were going to throw himself onto me. He talks and talks. Every time he leans forward I'm sure he's about to fall. He plays, feints, regains his balance, beats his wings, teeters, threatens to fall yet again, then recenters himself. It's all training, he says. Control. It's something you have to learn. He flaps, swings his hips, keeps talking. You have to close your eyes, he says, bending his knees, closing them.

I start to wonder how long the dance will last, what kind of tempo this is. The ritual is starting to bore me. Just as I'm about to go and leave him there, everything quickens. He lands beside me as lightly as he'd clambered up.

"This is Berkeley University. Ewe-see at Berkeley."

"I can see that."

Later we're at María and Roberto's apartment, sharing the bed with them, surrounded by rabbits. To the left, in a corner beside the window, is a pile of dirty clothes, where our hosts rummage every morning in search of the least-reeky garments. The room smells like old sweat and weed. When we wake up, we have to be careful not to step in the pools of urine the pets have left all over the floor. Scattered excrement, food. Days later, little brown pellets start to appear in my clothes. The rabbits and their trails have taken over everything.

My third and last memory from this time is a scene from Indian Rocks. A phosphorescent-green park full of massive gray and brown rock formations, enormous prehistoric sloths. Apart from the petrified stone animals, there's no one in sight. I can't feel my ears. Only the liquid streaming from my nose, the drops I wipe off and try to dry directly with pinched fingers. I rub my hands on my Lycra leggings. The edges of the rocks are sketched in silhouette against the electric sky. The only way to keep our hands warm is to shake them. Resting after every attempt, we rotate our wrists from side to side. We stretch our forearms. We stretch our fingers and palms, forming a downward lever with the other hand. My arms are numb. It hurts to stretch them. Rafael says that pain is pleasure and his great dream is to parachute off El Capitan. We climb up the boulders. We study the most challenging routes and give each other instructions.

"Now you. Foot here, right hand there, the other in this spot here. Now lift your foot. This hand in the crack, the other one here, then a dynamic. Push. That's it. Come up over the top. Long stretch with the right arm or you won't get there. Look if it helps. Good. Push hard. There you go. Try with this one. Keep going."

"I'm coming."

"I've got you."

"You've got me?"

"Come on, don't hold back."

I knew about El Cap because he carried it around on a beat-up postcard with soft, rounded corners. A thousand-meter granite wall with a heart carved into the whole center and a relief that looks like a nose, which is exactly what it's called.

The radiant wall materializes in my memory, always posing the same questions. How can rock possibly reflect light that way. The relationship between the truth and its exact moment of emergence. If the shape of what we see depends on conditions external to us, if the truth depends on the timing of its arrival or the angle of its perception. Does authenticity run on a schedule. Are there plausible or impossible ecosystems, depending on the window-pane, or on the light, better put, they're seen with. Why are there true places that seem false. Whether we can all live in absolutely any ecosystem, and what happens if we can't.

His friends said he had a drinking problem. That he got violent when he drank, and he drank often. That he wouldn't stop until he saw blood, his opponent's or his own, it didn't matter. He'd tear himself to pieces in the street for no reason at all, like a cowboy, or like how people in my country say cowboys fight: out of stubbornness or the need to show that they're macho men or that they can be. I'd heard that he and his girlfriend often came to blows, that she'd hit him and he'd bite her back, that they'd blast through bags of coke and end up attacking each other with their fists and their teeth. That she was a wild animal. That they'd cheat, that they'd get shitfaced and fuck anyone who crossed their path. That nobody ever said no; they were magnetic like that. Everyone would spread their legs for them. They'd believe the rumors about the other's infidelities (whether false or true, one thing or the opposite) and the slip or the suspicion would be paid in blood. In raw flesh.

That day, in the green-gray park, I decided to ask him if it was true. He frowned and stood up.

"Here's the deal with this boulder. I use this for support. You have to see if it works for you. If not, try this one," he said, climbing up to the triangular rock and sliding off along the edge in three seconds. "It's easy. You try it. Pay attention. Control."

That was our sport. Hunting for problems.

Our hands reddened, sensing the alchemy of chalk and sweat collected under our winter clothes, we sought shelter from the

wind behind the biggest boulder. We pulled out our dented thermos, coated in stickers, and drank some coffee. As we passed the
cup back and forth, I taped up a blister on the verge of bursting
and he sorted the pot seeds he'd been carrying in a candy tin with
no candy in it. It was phosphorescent, mossy, and typical of the
weed we'd buy from the Colombian guy; it left us jolted, electric,
our ears ringing after just three hits. Rafael talked, not looking at
me, as if to himself. Into his own compressed ears.

"If I drink from the bottle, that means a shitshow for sure.
Blood. That's what I've learned. I open a bottle, a bottle of anything,"
he said, growing more emphatic. His gaze was steady and grave,
his brow furrowed. "Of whatever, Julia. And I fucking lose it. I
have too much energy."

He continued with his task, filling another sheet of rolling paper and sliding his thumbs toward his spread fingers.

"Sometimes I feel like I can stop a moving train. I don't know
how to explain it. I get confused when I try."

I didn't say anything. His swollen, callused fingers—they
seemed stiff, almost deformed—worked with great care, caress-
ing the paper as he rolled it up and cinched the tobacco. A brick-
layer doing origami. His tongue flicked out. He finished sealing it.
He held it out to me with his arms stretched long, lowering his
head and looking down at my feet. There was a taut cord between
the two images: his rough body, his attentive bow. Two possibilities. I accepted the cigarette and returned the gesture. I played the
damsel's game. I lit it, aware of my own fascination with the strange
contrast, the rift between them. You keep living, you keep getting
to know yourself.

"All I know is that I don't fight anymore," he continued. "I take
it easy. I've learned how to go with the flow, as the gringos say."

I wondered if the bit about the train was true, if he really
thought he had superpowers. The childishness of the image struck
me now. He spoke as if he were eight, nine years old. I thought

about how flexibility and incongruity complement each other. Seen from outside, a body's movement along the rope is unsettling, improbable. The possible versions of the man before you are only troubling if you look at them warily from a distance. If you refuse the pact. Everyone's an evolving species. An endangered chameleon. A single tightrope from the day we're born till the day we die.

Thinking about inconsistency, I had to stand. Grit in my eyes. "Want to fly?' he asked me.

With his hands wrecked and the thermos empty, lying on his back in the grass with his legs stretched skyward like columns, he instructs me. I bend my knees and settle my back onto the palms of his hands and the soles of his feet. I move backward. His feet receive my lower back; I feel his fingers. I support my dorsal against his hands. I'm a bow, my chest opens out toward the clouds, my arms fall slack to each side. Dead limbs. I struggle to breathe; my lungs don't have room to inflate. I gasp, but it's just fear.

"Open your wings. Relax your wings."

I start breathing. I close my eyes. The fear evaporates. He folds me, massages my back with his soles and palms, turns me around, and I let him. My will is to have no will. A rush of air inward. The force that pulls you toward the undersoil is the same force that lifts you up. I see the color of the grass before me. I feel his limbs pressing into the bends of my body. I feel the weight of my inner thighs entrusted to his feet. I feel my armpits filling his hands. He travels the entire length of my body as he moves me. He turns me over twice more, like a vine. I'm a knot. He ties me and undoes me, he twists me and my vertebrae crack. I close my eyes every so often so I don't have to see what he's doing. So I don't have to know what I'm showing him. The line of my breasts. My ass. My lower abdomen announcing myself, two millimeters fleeing their Lycra toward the light. Everything passes. Your body doesn't matter when someone takes over your body. If you took charge of it yourself, you'd never let anyone touch you again. I'm floating and don't have to do anything. I'm a jellyfish. I grow into the four aquatic throbs he offers me as assurance. I'm an embryo swimming in my mother's belly. Rafael calls it flying. I call it diving, returning to the uterus. I'm a freediver, an amphibian. You have to close your eyes underwater. I'm a deep-sea creature. There's no light inside your body.

The cold and the fear had vanished; I'm not sure when. My eyelids parted. Every depth has its shore. Every precipice has its landscape. When he returned me to the surface, flexing his legs and placing me gingerly onto the ground, it was time to go.

"You're a natural."

I stayed there. Astonished by my trust, by my viscous submission, by the tingling in my lower abdomen despite the layers of clothes and the germinalness of everything. I took note. I accepted the photo, took up my new body, recognizing the part of me that was uncommanded, not even by myself. He gathered our things. The wind chilled my cheeks as it rose up from the city. This is the beginning, I thought suddenly and without explanation. Sometimes it happens that way. It's a matter of time. Every window has to open and show something. There are photos you understand long after looking at them for the first time. There are uncertain seeds. The first pages start to turn and that's when you know. Two days later my whole body still hurt. Like after a good fuck.

Soon after, I received a demonstration, a preview of the moving train plus the alcohol, too. I witnessed it in Caracas on the night of the DJ incident. We went to a party Lupe had invited us to; she was dating a guitarist and she'd beg us to come at every possible chance. Partly to share the next day's hangover, so she wouldn't be the only one climbing with a weight belt in La Guairita, but mostly so she wouldn't end up all alone in a dark corner of some club after dawn, not knowing where to even start looking for her rockstar, finding herself next to two drunks locked in their own personal porno, or alongside three cokeheads fighting over a shared bag. Her boyfriend was a popular guy. He'd stop to greet everyone and their mother every couple of steps, so if Lupe showed up without climbing buddies she'd have a lousy time. Anesthetized by alcohol, she'd end up in the middle of the dance floor or adrift in a hallway, anchorless, looking all around her. Suspended in the void. Until the guy showed up, or until her accidental company grew unbearable, or until she regained her faith and her strength and decided to keep looking. Once she found him going into the men's room with another dude.

"Fuck, I'm not sure if I saw what I think I did. It was just a second, I'm not sure."

She didn't want to tell me what she'd seen through the crack in the door. I only know it involved some pants pulled down, a paper bag, and a needle. Nothing in the vein, he'd promised from the beginning. That was their pact. Nothing in the vein.

The last night I went with her was the one that ended with Rafael and the train episode. We were on our way out. We'd gotten into Tomás's SUV and were only waiting for Lupe, in the passenger seat, who both made out furiously with the guitarist and fought with him through the window, showing no interest in saying goodbye.

"Okay, that's it! Get a room or fuck off!"

No matter how supportive you wanted to be, no one could stand their spectacle after the frenzy of the club, much less at that hour, feeling the burn of your own fried brain, sensing dawn's orange ache in your eyes. I should've fallen asleep, but if I closed my eyes

I'd vomit. Then Rafael slipped out through the car's back window, vaulting like a monkey from beside me onto the street, or like a leopard: swift, incredibly agile. And for no apparent reason—because except for Lupe's little scene, everything indicated that we were about to leave—he was in the middle of the road within a split second, moving against traffic, chasing the DJ, tackling him to the ground, kicking and punching. We were told later that he bit the guy's ear and it bled. Or maybe the guy himself shouted it from the sidewalk: "You bit my ear, you son of a bitch!"

I didn't see it; I'm not sure about the ear part. When Rafael got back into the truck, I couldn't find any red streaks on his clothes. If you witness a fight, everything happens in slow motion, you get goosebumps; you're safe, but you're sweating. You take sides without caring who's right or why. When were finally all there, Tomás slammed on the accelerator. Maybe we were fleeing something. We sped off, burning rubber.

"What the fuck, man, are you crazy? Are you gonna keep putting on these fucking shows? I've had it, man. Jesus." And then, after a silence: "You've got some balls."

"What did he do to you?" I asked in a whisper. Rafael looked at me with dilated pupils and an iron jaw. It was then that I noticed his hands: they were hurt, trembling. I'd never seen this particular spectacle, the emergency on the backs of his hands, his fingers, his fists still tight. Fingernails maybe digging into his palms. His tone of voice, the crack exposing a fear only partly overcome by the punches he'd dealt. People fight to shake off their fear. Better to get it all out in the open than to keep holding it in.

"That fucking fat guy owed me. If a guy talks shit you have to teach him a lesson."

That's it. Full stop. He said nothing more. In a few minutes my dizziness and nausea were gone.

"Man, I'm dropping you off first. I don't even want to look at you, okay," Tomás said to him. And then, jabbing his index finger into his temple, "You're sick in the head. What you are is fucked up in the head."

"Hey, who's up for hot dogs from the Portuguese food truck?" Rafael answered.

"Fuck hot dogs, man. You're fucking crazy."

That was the last thing I heard before resting my head on Rafael's thighs and succumbing to sleep.

I always thought of his incidents with everyone else as his business with everyone else—things that had nothing to do with me. As long as it's not with me, I'd tell myself, always imagining some reason for the violence. Only he can know, I'd think. It happened because of this or that or whatever. There was no tragedy or disorder; maybe it was all part of the same expectation. The same taut rope between two cliffs, threatening to abandon us in midair. The same evolution. The same chameleon. I think he stroked my back and my hair with his swollen hands, but maybe I dreamed it. When I woke up, I was home, it was almost six in the morning, and apart from Tomás there was nobody else in the car. ⌗

Chapter II

Carlos isn't a bad guy, but I never saw him much. My cousins' birthdays. Christmas, New Year's Eve, one of the two. Once we went to Disney World.

He took care of the basics. New jeans once in a while, a few monthly tuition payments, the occasional doctor's appointment. Boxes of crayons. A calculator. As he himself said, he didn't know how to reconcile his heartache over my mother with my own existence as his daughter, with his own continuity. He had issues with offspring.

"I couldn't handle you guys," he says. As if my mother and I had been a single entity, as if we were a tiny isolated ecosystem and our confinement had gradually rendered us an extinct species. Some ecosystems are as small as a fallen log. In the end it felt like my fault, or at least my burden, that my moron parents didn't love each other anymore.

"Seeing you is like seeing her," he'd say, trying to make excuses. Having me in front of him, taking me to the park or buying me an ice cream, answering my calls, were painful experiences for him, harmful. I was to blame for being her daughter as well as his own, for resembling them both. I had her eyes, his build. Her stubbornness, her tenacity. And, I guess, his need to escape.

You always need an alibi. First it was work. He was always busy inventing things. In those offices at the university, where everyone knew when he showed up but never how late he stayed or with who, he met a woman he ended up marrying before he even introduced me to her. My disinheritedness may have already been clear, but the university that was the girlfriend who became the wife was what dissolved my genetics altogether and for good. Carlos erased me. Eventually his two new kids appeared. Julia-implosion. Bam. No more daughter. He'd call me once in a while, still does occasionally. I suppose he'd call more often if I made it easier for him. But they were and remain pathetic, his badly timed attempts, his anachronistic questions, always about homework I'd already handed in, boyfriends I'd already forgotten, projects cut short. Peaks already climbed and trips I could no longer remember. Always telling me stories about siblings who aren't mine. He isn't a bad guy.

In the early years, he'd talk and I'd just wait for him to pause, to take a breath, so I could get away, not offering much: I have to study, Mom's calling me, I was just on my way out. Any excuse was a good excuse if it helped me end the call by saying as little as possible. At a certain point I'd hold the receiver as I thought about the next climbing route, the assignment due for school. Not listening. He isn't a bad guy but he doesn't know who I am. And it's not easy to forgive estrangement. That kind of internalized abandonment is no joke. Every so often he'd show up at home with an invention, a tightrope walking-clown you had to wind up to make it slide along a wire, a clock that was a sun during the day and turned into a moon at six p.m. and which soon grew disoriented, so that multiple times a day it would change celestial bodies, planets, whatever you call it. A rock climber whose papier-mâché rock swiftly disintegrated, so that he climbed into the air.

"It's time to take care of things. All this piled-up stuff. Lots of boxes in this house. Lots of memories," he said the last time I saw him. "You have to be strong," he felt inspired to add.

"Better be on the lookout," I answered. Shot back. "There are boxes of yours, too. There must be boxes of yours."

There isn't much to say. I barely know him. I've kept some photos from vacations he invited me on with his family, photos where he doesn't appear at all; he must have been behind the camera. In one photo, I'm wearing my favorite skirt, the patchwork one my grandmother made and which I kept wearing for years because the waist was elastic and so it grew with me. My expression is serious. I'm in a park, not looking into the lens, leaning against the trunk of a palm tree, with an Indian shoulder bag slung across my torso. You can't see the leaves on the tree. In another photo, blurry, overexposed, I'm alone again, dazzled; it looks like I'm smiling, but I know I'm just screwing up my face to protect my eyes from the sun. I've got a stuffed Mickey Mouse tucked under my arm and there's a fountain behind me. Otherwise, there are two or three photos with his family. I'm never in the same place; I have no regular spot. His kids are always close to their mother, the boy to her left, the girl to her right. I'm on the outside, a little farther away from the adjacent arm, with a faraway gaze, looking for something beyond the camera that looks back at me.

It was different with my mom. She was pragmatic, trustworthy, consistent. She always saved everything. She saved my first tooth so she could disparage the ritual, disparage herself. "What poor taste," she'd say occasionally. "I'm like a cannibal, a savage. Whatever. This tooth is going to rot anytime now." But she never threw it away. She saved everything, everything. My drawings from kindergarten, lots of photos. Clothes, all of them. "It'll be back in style anytime now." My report cards. My hair bows, more photos, my elementary school folders. She worked from eight to eight. She was bossier than a general and I wasn't much better, I guess, because I never let myself be bossed around. I often left the house, with and without permission. I traveled as much as I could whenever I wanted. But when you're an only child, and in my mother's house I was, it's like you never leave. There's an unbreakable bond. An elastic band that everything else is built on, a slightly fragile connection, slightly tense, nonnegotiable. Permanent. Exhausting. I was always afraid of orphanhood, and to remedy this I made myself an orphan before my time.

They tell you the illness is here or it's there, and then suddenly it moves, it's not there anymore, or not only there. It's a mutating map. First in one place, then in three more, somersaulting from one spot of putrefaction to the next, sketching domes in disintegration. Eventually you stop asking and explaining. You don't waste time naming wherever the stain is now, and don't do it mostly because you're afraid of worsening the situation by even mentioning its festered existence. It was just the two of us, so I walked on eggshells.

What I can say is both minimal and a commonplace. Everyone dies of cancer now. We all know how it goes: first the doubts, the nagging discomforts. Then the bad news and a few blank days, then the tightrope. A future attached to a tightrope can be stretched if you apply the proper weight. Or that's what you think. That's the trap. You start to do everything. If you'd always skimped on vegetables, you change your diet. If you'd never exercised before, you rev into action. You try to relax if you'd been stressed, you follow your treatment plan like a soldier. Of course, if you put too much pressure on the cord, you ricochet, you're shot back into the cosmos. Same thing if you rush to reach the other side, if you're desperate to save yourself.

"I understand. But I don't get why this is happening to you. Don't get me wrong, I do wonder—what was it I didn't teach her? I don't know. But I understand. I mean, I can tell. It's hard for you."

"All these plans, Mom. Grocery lists, vacations, career choices, job, kids, love, old age. Everything. A board game. A plan for everything."

"People plan what they can when they can, Julia. Look at yourself in this mirror. I wish I could plan now but I can't."

"I think it's awful."

"But life isn't worthwhile without it, sweetie. We're not animals, Julia. You live in the clouds. I don't know why you don't see it. When I was your age I already had you."

"Things were different then. You say so yourself."

"I know."

"You're the one who's all long-live-the-future. If I ask Carlos, he says long live the present. That the future is impossible to scientifically prove. Please."

"You bring up Carlos whenever it suits you. Don't bring him up. He has nothing to do with this."

"Doesn't he? Who cares. What I'm saying is that if you plan things you're wasting your time, and if you dare to stop planning the train leaves you behind. You end up suspended in midair, as you put it, with no wings and no safety net. But just look at yourself."

"What am I supposed to look at?"

The nurse came in with a tray. She left it in on the bedside table. She wrote something on the clipboard at the foot of the bed and walked out again without a word. I lifted the edge of the plastic lid and rolled the table toward her.

"Grilled chicken and white rice. Broth. Jell-O. I don't get why they won't let me bring you food."

"It's probably fine. I'd rather have this than one of your concoctions," she said, smiling for the first time all morning.

"Oh, I'm sure you would," and I smiled, too. "Anything but my concoctions. Open wide."

"Better dead than drenched in blood. I'll do it myself," she responded shortly, reaching for the fork.

We went through the final stretch together: the gauntness and pain, the swelling, the weakness, the baldness, a selective amnesia of who knows what. We'd smile resignedly at each other. Your mother dies and you relearn how to live. You start digging into your memory and imagining conversations that never happened and yet you can't go on without. Moments return that you were sure you'd already coped with. Everything hurts all over again and it's a rancid, heavy pain, incurable. I found myself alone when I was sick, when I was getting better, when I was trying to mend. I found myself alone in seclusion, hibernating, and as I tried to move on. I stopped cooking. I never sat down again in the chair where she'd sat to stare out at the landscape in the late evening. Now I wonder what she thought about, sitting there, and if any part of her silence was about me. Sometimes I'd hear her in the bathroom and it sounded like she was crying. I know there was no question that would make a difference, that the answer would be just another argument, another irony. In the face of silence, better not to speak at all. Living under the same roof with those kinds of doubts—it's no joke. When it was all over, I couldn't stay.

In the very last days, it felt like death was seated on the couch in her bedroom, waiting. Like a guest who won't leave even when you refuse him coffee, lean a broom against the door, turn out the lights, shout that it's time to go. Mom started to see her own destruction, and not just because of the pain, which was predictably intensifying. An encounter with the mirror told her the real story. It whispered everything that was about to happen into her ear. She didn't want to die. With her hair she lost her hope, started talking about bodies and worms and cremation. Then a fine fuzz rose on her scalp, which she covered with a scarf and never got the chance to grow out, as she quipped, into decent, God-given hair. The baby chick-fluff, the deterioration, revealed her peripheral place in the course between cancer and medicine. Nurses and doctors came in and out, explaining nothing. They'd jot down milligrams and times of day on the clipboard. At most, they'd smile. Meanwhile, she'd feel her scalp, fluffing her fluff upward, as if she had something else to put there instead.

"I love your hair that way," she'd say, who knows why, because I don't often get my hair cut, and even less in the trance-state I was in. "I want mine like that, too. When do you think I could go?"

Right when I'd decided not to tell her any details about the progression of her illness, she stopped looking at herself in the mirror. She asked me to do her makeup, so she wouldn't have to see herself. I'm certain that when she leaned into the reflection over the bathroom sink, she faced, apart from her own stark skull, the vision of the same rotted webs I couldn't stop looking at, either.

Eventually our friends would ask after her and her prognosis and I'd say something just to say something. In the end, when it comes to certain anatomical matters, anatomy doesn't matter. The only important and hypocritically irreversible thing, despite all the pills, amid all the vomit, was in plain sight: life being lost bit by bit. A nocturnal coup, even if it happened in broad daylight. An off-beat, disproportionate collapse: three days better, one day awful, keeping us on constant guard.

Once, in the middle of the night, I opened my eyes and saw that she wasn't in bed. I jolted, first assuming it was all over, then thinking they must have changed her to a different room, realizing at the same time that it was impossible for anything to have happened without my noticing, since we slept (or didn't sleep) less than a meter away from each other. I ran out into the hall, my steps both quick and clumsy. Like a bear. I found her alone in the half-lit corridor. Another bear. A nightmare, I told myself. I'm having a nightmare. But nobody woke me up to shake me out of it. When I approached her, she didn't let me get in a word.

"The car keys. Do you have them? We'll be late," she said in a thick voice, slurring.

I started paying attention to how she drank water, how she held her fork. Whether she trembled. At first she'd squint to focus on the TV. Then she'd ask us to lower the volume because she couldn't identify the characters and wasn't interested in the shows. I'd concentrate on which childhood memories she could recover and which were slipping away from her. I'd try to understand the grenades falling into her memory, try to describe to myself what was exploding in those fields I'd always found so mysterious; what was coming apart and why. One afternoon I found her snipping at her pajamas with a cuticle cutter because I needed a new skirt.

"What will Carlos say if he sees you with your patchwork skirt all faded like that? He's going to think you don't have what you need. He'll think I can't give it to you."

I started keeping watch, searching for meaning in laughable details that didn't make any sense and weren't actually funny at all. First came the drop in energy, then the loss of physical composure, and then, finally, a fickle clarity. There were moments when Mom knew where she'd left her glasses, put together jigsaw puzzles or block towers without any trouble, like an adult. And then she'd suddenly attack her own fingernails in a rage, using the bed sheet to rub off the polish I'd painted on her the day before: "That woman did a terrible job. I'm going to fix it."

At first I was hopeful, a stance I thought was worthwhile. When I realized what was coming, I stopped counting the days. I'd sleep at strange hours. I didn't eat much. I started avoiding the stains and my own obsession with the trails she left like sticky cobwebs. I'd spend hours telling her my favorite childhood memories. About the times she'd taken me to the park and we'd ride the seesaw. Beach vacations with my aunt Elizabeth and Eloísa. I'd talk for hours in the middle of the night about how eagerly I'd wait for her to pick me up from school, how I'd boast about her to my friends. "My mom is the prettiest," I told her I'd tell them. You only talk about the good things when you're aware of the bad all around you. I'd tell her the same anecdotes until she fell asleep. I wish I could have taken her to nap in the sun. Life passes quickly. I like to imagine she died in one of those swings.

Then it was all tightropes and travel. When everything is dancing and pressing into the void, in the right-now, in the *this*, you have to give it all you've got. You have to learn. That's what I thought. Everyone learns however they can. *Poof.* Existence: gone. Just like that. Things get left behind. Closetfuls of things. Bedrooms full of accumulated years. You open a drawer and get dizzy. You find yourself. A tooth. A hair-tie. A postcard. That's the worst part. You find your mother's version of yourself. What you could have been. 🐟

CHAPTER III

"You can't see it yet, but we're the same, you and me. Don't you get it?" he once asked me. We were sitting on my living room couch, and we barely knew each other in person. All we'd done by then was write each other two or three letters a month after my first stay in Berkeley, where we met. He came to Caracas and called me up. He got into a cab, unshowered, and rang the buzzer.

"Very nice to meet you, ma'am. Rafael, at your service," he said to my mother, bowing his head as humbly as an Andean farmer.

She said nothing. She let him in. Then she'd keep appearing in front of us over and over, watching us sidelong. That look of hers. Mouth pursed, lips pressed together, corners lightly etched. Those two vertical lines sunk between her eyes.

He asked me the question and stared at me, incredulous, amused. "You really don't see it?"

As if I'd just confessed I couldn't recognize the color blue, I'd never taken a bus in my life, or I'd started college without ever reading a single book. I studied the look on his face and thought: one, my friends were right. Rafael lived on a different planet. Two, he was arrogant and rude. Or three, the guy could see and I was blind. I didn't care which of the three possibilities was true.

We met out-of-synch: when the postcard said he was headed off to climb El Capitan, he'd already come back down and was carousing on some Californian beach. By the time he received my postcard about some final exam, I was already on break. We knew the same people, had places in common. But we experienced them differently. I was living with my mom and I worked at the university library. He lived wherever, with his parents or in Mérida or in La Guairita. He'd refer to normal people sarcastically, with scorn. When he wanted to get on my nerves, he'd say, "You normal people take yourselves so seriously. Bullshit. You think you're so important just because you wear a damn watch. Who says you have to eat three meals a day? Just because *you* eat three meals a day, everyone else has to stuff their faces all the time? I know you don't get it. None of you gets it."

"So it turns out we're pretty different after all, right?" I'd reply. "I stand corrected. Now it's you and us. You and us. That's right."

Sitting beside him on the couch, I stared at the climbing cord he used to keep his black acetate glasses from falling to the ground. They'd plummeted down to the surface of the planet so many times that they were now permanently warped, and the only way he could keep them gripping his skull was this one: with a cord tightened hard around it. He forced himself to see: to see, he needed a climbing cord pulled tight to his skull. To have any vision at all, he needed that slender cord around his head. Fascinated and vaguely repulsed, I stopped listening and focused instead on this particular hobo-like part of him, this faulty way of existing in the world. Fearing my typical fondness for the broken and the insufficient, I wondered whether I liked what I saw in Rafael, and how much like me he really was. There was something. I was seeing something through his battered glasses. Deep down, I didn't know him beyond the fantastical stories he'd dole out to me—the tales that reached my doorstep in envelopes, or through messengers, or through the stories our mutual friends used to tell me. According to them, you had to make your way through a lot of fear to get anywhere near him. But I was never afraid, as if I had nothing to lose. Or as if we were siblings. That's how natural it felt.

"Which is why I'm saying that we're creatures from the same puddle. You know all about that—aren't you supposed to be a biologist? A puddle contains all kinds of creatures. You should know."

That night, shadowed by a lioness who circled us incessantly and watched us with her furtive eyes, Rafael reassured me and convinced me. We hadn't yet really seen each other. We hadn't been living in sync with each other, and we didn't even have much in common. But there he was, on my living room couch, prattling on about the origins of the species that connected us.

I couldn't entirely let my guard down. There was something dubious, something fragile about him—a clumsily adjusted cord. It's one thing to love traveling and long to escape. It's another thing altogether to wander the world without a change of clothes, dirty, giving away whatever you've got left over when you've got absolutely nothing left over at all. To survive by fishing food out of dumpsters and laughing about it. Evaluating dumpsters by the quality of the restaurant they belong to, the type of food, the status of the clientele. Begging for money or stealing it, whatever you have to do, so long as the trip never ends. It's one thing to climb; it's another to choose walls that will destroy you unless you make it to the top. This is what I was thinking about that night on the couch. I even could have argued about it. "How alike could we really be, Rafael?" I could have asked him. But I just sat there and looked at him. In my silence was an acceptance, a pact. For some reason—or, better put, without any logical reason at all—I believed in the existence of a shared code that would allow us to travel from one part of the ecosystem to another, cross the border between one life and the other, and discover that just a couple strokes could bring us to the same place in the water: the same spot in the same puddle. We could have the same shadow. I didn't understand it, didn't see where we overlapped. But I wasn't worried about being wrong. If it all went to hell, that's because it had to.

Less than three weeks before, he'd come to Berkeley. That's when we inaugurated our own form of time—which is linked with space, after all. We came to calculate how long we'd been together in two different ways, together-together or together-apart. Adding up trips we took together and the times we overlapped in Caracas, we had been together for about two years. Together but apart, nearly seven. Together-together, we traveled to seven countries on three continents. In three countries on two continents, we fought, and although we arrived together, we left apart.

These days, people can't handle delays in the arrival of any kind of news. Travel and distances feel like skips and jumps. Everything is now. Any silence longer than an hour suggests that something terrible has happened: you've been forgotten, the silent person is dead, he never really loved you. If he doesn't write you back right away, or if you don't receive what he wrote you right away, there's no doubt about it: he doesn't love you anymore. People aren't willing to wait, and when they have to, they get offended. Although I constantly yearned for news that never came, or which arrived when I least expected them, I'd convince myself. I'd describe the landscapes to myself, I'd mentally visit or invent faraway highways, endless roads and paths, cliffs, hundred-meter walls. Places where a phone or a computer would be a cartoon, a joke. I'd visit and invent these places, and I'd also revisit thoughts of our love and companionship to keep from worrying. When you have to wait for a long time, you're accompanied by what hasn't arrived because it can't. A completeness. Faith, if you like. A love of silence. Anyone who consciously waits for delayed news learns how to wait with a sense of wholeness. So I managed to stay whole, waiting. Because I feared knowing, maybe. You don't ask for what you know no one will give you. Better dead than drenched in blood.

"I can't make any other kind of commitment. I can't give you anything else. This is what I can offer you. And I can't handle seeing you cry. So if this doesn't work for you, I understand. But we'd better draw the line here. I care too much to see you like this, Bird." Those were the usual exit strategies, when he'd catch me feeling sad or unsure. "Bird, I really can't stand it when you cry. You don't deserve this."

Hasta la vista, baby. That sort of thing. You either get with the program or they leave you and it's your fault. You asked for it. That's what you get for being so demanding. You eventually figure out that if you want the guy, you have to stay put. At the same time, something told me that Rafael, without his train and his taboo bottles and his deadly walls and his disappearances, was nothing. Left of zero. A zombie. It wasn't just that I couldn't change him; it's that it wasn't worth trying. So I went for it. The whole package.

Every traverse is the same. It's the same meditation every time, the same acid sweat. And they're always different: they change with the weather; the rock is more or less adhesive depending on the temperature. When it's cold, your shoes stick more. They change with your mood and how many people are around, if there's anyone around, or depending on how much time you've got to finish. All you need is a bag of chalk and your climbing shoes. That's it. You approach the rock, rotate your joints, your wrists, elbows, shoulders, ankles. You stretch. You bend forward, try to touch your toes. You extend your fingers, hide your regular shoes under a bush or in a little cave. Maybe that's also where you leave your car keys, if you drove, and you cover them with leaves. You pull on your climbing shoes. You try to step lightly. They're so tight that your nails dig into your cuticles, and the pain is almost unbearable until they go numb. You have to try to float. Everything happens within five or ten minutes; nothing hurts once you're up there. You only feel the stinging again at the end, when you come down off the rock and start to walk. But what does it matter then—the job's already done.

At the foot of the wall, you slip one hand into the chalk bag tied around your waist, then the other. Ready. You grasp one hold. Then another. You lift one foot, press hard into the rock, then lift the other, and you're set. You make your way from the hole-ridden wall where you made your ascent toward a slab at the edge of a cliff, at the end of the bluff. You pass caves and overhangs. You clasp at small, sharp-edged crystals and at vanilla-colored mini-buttes. Those are smoother; they look like the cartilage of some alien creature, colossal kneecaps. You insert your hands into pockets, into cracks; you adjust your palms, your wrists; you stick your arms in up to your elbows if you have to. You support yourself on ridges and shelves. You travel.

Everything depends on your chosen route. La Guarita has its own cosmography. You know where to change your clothes, where to nap or pee, where to work on your speed or technical steps or finger-strength. The spots allocated for each task have their own names, and they're unmistakable; they have their own public and private histories. You can reach almost all of them on foot. To do so, you have to navigate rocks, leap across small drops, pass nooks and crannies that a new arrival could barely distinguish at all. You have to access some of the caves by climbing vertically; you can't make them out from the ground. Buzzard's Hollow, Ahimsa, The Wall, The Vagina, Nutella, Close to the Edge.

Your hands swell during the first few months. Blisters and bubbles cover your fingers before they burst and cede to callus. These injuries, and eventually the scars and leathery skin, are trophies you display as proof of your work on the wall. The tougher your hands, the more prepared you are to support yourself with smaller or sharper holds.

There are as many traverses as there are climbers. Rafael goes as high as possible; the grips are big and comfortable there. Foolproof. But if you fall from all the way up there, a broken ankle or shoulder is a best-case scenario. You only need to remember what

climb closer to the ground. Down below, ll and the walls are overhangs. It's more . Harder but safer. Some climbers finish inutes; some of us take nearly an hour. three. Some come down to rest along the ult steps. Others take pride in not touching some climbers, the traverse finishes where ey return on foot. For others, it's forbidden hey have to climb there and back without find themselves where they first went up. y. Sometimes you climb accompanied, chat- nter the park at dawn so you can hear the se fog parting around your steps. The park d your feet stick better. Everyone has their re a different story: you need a harness, a d at least one rope partner. You can't climb sometimes you wouldn't want to. A traverse gether; it's the temple, as Aquilino used to say. La Guairita first thing in the morning, when That's ideal. After the traverse, you go direct- e going. With chalk residue under your nails l on your skin. People can't even figure out like.

pleasure," says Tomás. The first time I heard climbed before going to college, I found him both lazy and pretentious. Tomás talked as if he knew secrets that were inaccessible to mere mortals, as if he'd decided to share them

with you out of the goodness of his heart, not expecting you to understand. His vanity was obvious, but I never contradicted him. No one, better put, ever contradicted him. He'd use that condescending tone when he talked about raw food (*pura vida*, he'd say), or about how heavy his homemade vegan energy bars turned out: "You might think they're heavy at first, but that's because you're not used to eating healthy. Soon you'll feel light as a feather, you'll see."

"But they give me diarrhea."

"Fiber is important. Give it a week or two and you'll see."

He'd use that tone, too, to expound on the benefits of waking up before dawn: "With the birds and the squirrels—it's the most natural way." On the benefits of fasting: "There are people who only ingest water and *prana*. That's all you need." Or when he'd distribute his yogurt starter cultures without even asking if we wanted them: "Take care of these. Don't let them die on you this time." He'd use it when he discussed the different kinds of cheeses made with sieves: "Yeah, with a sieve—you know what a sieve is, don't you? Eight hours in a sieve in the sink, and *voilà*: the only cheese that's tolerable to human digestion." And he'd use it to justify his morning climbs or his absences in class. He was studying biology, like me, but his concentration was in botany and he graduated before I did. On the day of the ceremony, toga and mortarboard and all—"My scientist costume"—he brought five boxes of books to school. "Academia is a waste of time. Air is my thing. Life is my thing. None of this is useful to me anymore," he said, dropping the last box onto the floor. And, turning to me: "Don't you worry, princess. I've got you covered. There's more in the car if you want them."

Now he runs a factory that makes granola and raw vegan cookies. After all his endlessly sticky trial runs, business is good, and he's upheld his own principle: first obligation, then pleasure. As for the box of books he left me, I used them all: I barely had to photocopy anything all the way through school. It was Tomás, Fabián,

Rafael, Lupe, and me. Out of all the possible outcomes, the only thing I couldn't have imagined was that one of us would leave the community we were or believed ourselves to be. That's what families are: the illusion that only death is strong enough to break the ties that bind you. ▦

Chapter IV

Sector B is a kind of limbo. Sector A doesn't exist and neither does C. Sector B is a subset of nothing. It's a parenthesis with nothing outside it, a parallel ecosystem for loners.

We don't talk. The park is closed, so we jump the fence. The ground is still wet at that hour and the gray rocks shine like old silver. The damp leaves skid under our shoes. We walk with our eyes on the ground, uttering monosyllables in low voices. It's like we're trying not to break something, trying to let natural history evolve alongside us in the frame. Lizards. Bats. Macaws. Squirrels. Sloths. We walk gingerly, trying not to wake anyone. We make our way into the limbo with two ideas in mind. Synchronicity is one of them. We have our gear. It smells like eucalyptus. You can't shout on the mountain, you can't make any noise. I unfurl the rope, take out the gear, pull on my harness. Rafael rolls a joint. Lights it. No one speaks. Shoes, belay device. Chalk. I blow the excess off my right hand. Hands and one foot on the vertical. Before lifting the other, I turn, raise my eyebrows, and nod.

"Good."

To climb, you keep your pelvis close to the rock, as if you wanted to go in—to open up the wall and go in. Your thighs heat and tremble. Your palms sweat. You have to keep breathing as you go, shake out your arms; all the gripping and clenching leave them taut as drums. You let go with one arm and hang from the other, moving the one you released so the blood starts flowing again. Then you change your grip and shake out the other arm. If you don't, eventually you won't be able to close your fist at all. Same with breathing. If you don't breathe, you'll turn into a rubber doll, stiff, obtuse. A robot. When you know how to breathe you're just another tree branch, a lizard.

You pull the rope with one hand, and depending on how much you need to pass it through the carabiner, you hold it in your mouth, clamping it between your teeth as you keep pulling. You support yourself on the wall with a single hand. You reel in more rope. You thread it through the carabiner and continue sewing the wall once you've secured it. You keep climbing upward. You look all around you and invent a map in your head. Focusing, you see a ledge in the distance. You climb a little higher. It's when you grab on or position your foot that you know the slab or the quartz will support you. One limb at a time. One pause at a time. You're practicing.

"What do you mean by *plan*, Mom?" I'd tell her. "Life is all practice, and if you mess up you might bomb it, it's true. Or you might not."

We climb Synchro up to the ledge, up to the hotel, and we sit along the rope looking out into the precipice, swinging our legs. It's a big hotel. The treetops below us, the city. Blue before us. There we are. Eating an orange. Our fingers sticky with juice and chalk, dirt and sweat. Masters of a time when nothing was happening and everything was yet to happen.

He turns to me. He looks at me like a bird, with his head tilted and his eyes both curious and empty. He takes my jaw into his citrus-smeared hands. He pushes me, pulls me backward. Inward. The film starts to roll. The planet with its people and horizontal landscapes are suddenly far away. Chest inflamed with so much breath. Diaphragm crushed by a body that isn't mine but seems like it. Bird, you don't realize it, but you and I are exactly the same. A fissure swallowing his voice and my memory. His snail tongue, my grass body, his vertigo sex. He undid the braid in my hair. He grabbed a lock and yanked it; I felt my neck stretch. The nape pulled back. It's like he wants to drown me, I thought, as if the dead woman were someone else. I can't control myself. I remembered the sentence and then I told myself, as if I were watching someone else's movie: that's it. It's time to know.

I wrapped my legs around him. My hair tangled with the twigs and dry leaves serving as our bed. I became a carnivorous plant. He fastened me, he carried me like a feather, I can stop a moving train, as if I were almost nothing and this meant he could do whatever he wanted with me. It wasn't the first time it's happened and it won't be the last: sometimes I think I'm going to die and I don't care. Maybe I'm about to die, and I don't care, I thought suddenly, astonished, discovering a new part of myself, as he sustained me and entered me, liquid that I had become.

"Before this is all over I'm going to fuck you in every cave in this park. In every single one, you hear me? Before this is all over," he said again, a warning, with no trace of a smile. I decided not to look at him. We gathered our gear, rappelled down, and kissed at the bottom. Saying little else, we left, me to my place and he to his. That night I spent a long time untangling my hair and pulling leaves and grass from the knots.

Two days later, after climbing up a drenched, muddy traverse, I sat on a boulder facing Relámpago. Wiping the sole of my boots on my pants so I could clean off at least a little silt before returning them to my pack, I heard his voice behind a couple curves. I stayed there, not waiting for him, which is how you wait for people who avoid being waited for, evasive people, bird people, cat people.

By then it was clear that what happened at the hotel hadn't changed anything else at all. It made no difference if Rafael escaped along the green paths. Fabián and Tomás approached, jumping from boulder to boulder without a glance at their feet, grazing roots, barely touching the ground where it was slickest. Fabi was telling a story, mimicking someone and gesturing wildly. They smelled of something acidic and sweet, dust, bat guano, wet earth, sweat, weed, a mission accomplished.

"Fucking horror movie, man."

"Nothing but mud."

"Black and Decker."

Black and Decker is an expression of Tomás's. Black: dark. Scary. But since you have to laugh at what scares you, it's Black and Decker. The name of a household appliance in a place like La Guairita, it makes you laugh. Black and Decker: inoculation against fear. Rafael and Caboose appeared a couple minutes later. Same smell. When he sat beside me, his chalk bag fell to the ground, spitting dust and a white crystal from Roraima that he always brought with him, an amulet. He pulled out the stub of a joint and lit it.

"They're inviting me to La Gran Sabana," he said, holding the air in his lungs, signaling toward them with his mouth shut and a slight nod, eyebrows raised, chest obviously burning, about to explode. "They have room in the truck," he said as he finally exhaled.

He passed me the joint. I breathed in, calculating when they might have invited him, after the hotel or before. I'd never know. I inhaled again, wanting to burn up the rest of the stub, turn it to ash.

"And this would be when?"

"Tomorrow morning, really early."

Shit.

"And you have everything ready? You haven't stocked up."

"They're taking care of it, Bird. All I have to do is decide if I want to go. They have extra food and they're going to pay. The royal treatment."

He took a final drag, handed me the joint, and got to his feet.

"Just have to pack up and all set," he said with a glance at me, furrowing his forehead and shifting his gaze to the ground. He blew out what he'd held in. He passed a hand over my hair, barely touching me. Tilted head. Empty eyes. Creased brow. Looking at me again, gravely, he opened his mouth to say something.

"Ready, Tomás?"

You're not fucking serious.

He looked at Tomás, turned his face back to me once more, and gave me a kiss on the forehead that landed on my scalp.

"Let's go, Tom."

The *hasta-la-vista-baby* factor. Before they got into the truck, Tomás bowed, Fabi mimicked an *I'll call you*, Caboose flashed a V with the index and middle fingers of his right hand. Rafael blew me a kiss. I tossed the joint to the ground, stood up, and listlessly attempted the first steps of Relámpago. I made my way down the boulder in a couple movements, the strength gone from my hands, overpowered by the image of my body falling face-up onto the sharp rocks, imagining my head like a watermelon. It must be horrible to get your skull smashed in an empty park. I left.

Two days later, Fabi and El Gocho and I were in La Puerta, eleven hours from Caracas, unloading the truck and getting ready to climb a 250-meter canyon path over a river where all you could hear was the water rushing through itself on its journey to who knows where. When we felt the first drops of what would swiftly become a tropical downpour, we were finishing the first pitch. We completed the ascent and set up the rappel. The rope was immediately drenched and caked with mud; it almost didn't pass through the curves of the figure-eight. You had to push off with your feet to help yourself down and peel away from the bluff. "Rock! Careful! Rock!" we'd yell, knowing that the only audible sound below was the river and recognizing the futility of our attempts to protect any human being who strangely happened to be walking along the bank in the middle of a storm. When we reached the bottom, we rolled up the rope, leaden with water, and headed straight for the house.

The house was a mud-walled shack with a dirt floor that we were renting from an old man named Pascual. It was about a fifteen-minute walk through the woods from the town, and it was the only place with a roof and space for up to eight hammocks, a ledge for our packs and gear, and another for our food and cooking equipment. We almost always traveled with two- or three-burner cooking stoves, gas and kerosene.

The river was a choppy sea. El Gocho knotted his rope to his harness and slung it around a tree to make a pulley. Fabián also roped himself to the harness and started to cross.

"I'm going!"

I'm going, he said, and fell in. We couldn't see him. We shouted his name as if it would somehow help him to hear us, as if our voices could get him upright and out of the water. I screamed as if to beg him: "Fabi, I'm here! We're right here!" Our eyes searched the current as if spotting a hand or a piece of backpack amid the river's wild rush would be of any use. According to what he told us later, he never heard our yells. At one point he could tell he was dying, and without knowing which end was up, he pushed his feet against something solid and shoved himself forward, enraged, with all the strength he could muster, knowing it was his only chance. That was when his head emerged and he regained his balance, grabbed hold of a tree trunk, and pulled himself along until he reached the other side, breathless. Black and Decker. Stuff that happens. Supposedly it doesn't. But it does. When he'd adjusted the rope on the other side, I followed.

"I got you! Relax, I got you!" he said, pulling to help me across while El Gocho tightened the rope from behind. I took off my shoes so I could feel the bottom better—that's what Fabi recommended after his slip—and tied them to the top of my pack. When I finished crossing, they were gone.

Once we were on the other side, El Gocho offered to carry his girlfriend's backpack, but she wouldn't let him. She took two steps backward. I don't know what she said, but she nearly spat at him. Fabi and I lit two Belmonts. Tobacco kills, but it's a nice ritual after not dying.

"Nice job, man," Fabi said to El Gocho, giving him a little pat on the back. You're doing fine, Gocho, keep going, he was saying with the pat. Atta boy. Apparently El Gocho and the girl had been dating for a while, but for some reason they hadn't fucked yet. You could tell that the poor guy was going for broke.

"All these bastards think you'll spread your legs if they get to carry your fucking backpack," she said when I caught up with her. I thought this was a little much. El Gocho was following with Fabi, the rope strung around his torso from shoulder to waist like a Miss Universe sash, his eyes on the ground, calling out to her occasionally. She wouldn't answer.

"Isn't that sort of harsh?" I said. "Say something to him. Besides, he's pretty hot—what do you have to lose?"

"You fuck him if you like him so much," she answered.

"Hey, no, what's the matter with you? That's crossing a line," I said. Fear exposes the animal we all carry around inside us.

"Drop it, then."

"That's crossing a line," I insisted, and added as a warning, "Don't push your luck."

"Time for lentils!" Fabi shouted, and then said to El Gocho, loud enough for us to hear, "The princesses are hurrying up because they want all the food for themselves! Come on, dude, better get a move on or there won't be any left for us."

I slowed down and waited for them. Those were the last words I exchanged with the girl from Mérida. We didn't speak to each other in the hours that followed and I never saw her again. When we reached the house, it was already dark. We wolfed down the food. I pulled three big chocolate bars out of my backpack and they instantly disappeared. No one spoke, except for the occasional comment about how stupid it would have been to die right there in the river. There are deaths and then there are deaths. When we'd finished, Fabián stacked the dishes and went out shirtless toward the river. His pants slung low across his hips, his broad shoulders balancing the cooking pots and dirty plates. You don't know many muscles are in the back, how many lines it sketches as it moves, until you see a rock climber's back. His tattoo wasn't showing, the one on his hip, but I knew where to look for it along the bottom edge of that sun-browned torso that I stood to follow.

I took a few steps, but I stopped short mid-path. I watched him melt into the brush. I walked back toward my hammock and settled in to sleep before he returned.

"Watch it, guys, you're being way too obvious," I heard the girl from Mérida say later from inside her hammock, veiled by her mosquito net. "Better put out the blunts, Pascual's probably coming."

No one responded; they carried on with their quiet music and their conversation or their secrets. The smoke and the smell of family seeped into the house, into my clothes. The light from the fire intensified the density of the ochre cloud around us. After a little while, El Gocho called out to her: "Come on, pretty lady, smoke this joint over here with me."

No answer. That was the last I heard until a sound awoke me, a rustle of fabric, creaking ropes, someone's breath. From my hammock I could see El Gocho moving inside his chrysalis. His hammock tensed at both sides and along the length of it. My immediate reaction was to turn toward the girl from Mérida. And there she was, in her own hammock, apparently asleep; I could see her feet and a lock of hair. Gocho didn't take long. After a few moments, I heard a sigh and he slipped out of his cocoon, tying the drawstring on his sweatpants. I didn't see him come back. I touched myself under my clothes. Wet. I thought of the image from a couple hours earlier. Of how I'd longed to follow Fabián to the river. The two guests were gone by daybreak. I didn't ask, but I learned later that they'd traveled to El Páramo in two different buses.

That day I devoted myself to untangling the belts and laying out some of our gear on the floor to dry. Mud had encrusted the fibers of the rope, plugged the belays. My clothes were soaked and smelled of fear. Old man Pascual passed in front of the house with his walking stick, a polished, barkless cane that retained the natural curves of its life as a tree. He always came by to make sure everything was all right, and he always appeared when I was alone. He lifted his hat when he saw me.

"Morning, little miss."

"Don Pascual, how are you? How is everything at home?"

"Fine, fine, out for a stroll. Making sure that everything is back in God's right place after the downpour. Making sure the house still has four walls. Lots of leaks?" he asked, checking the corners of the roof from underneath and examining the mud partitions. "Careful, little miss, you hear? Be careful out there. This river's carried off more than a couple folks, see."

He knocked his cane lightly against the wall. He peeled a fine thread from the bamboo and inspected it. "It has no mercy, this river. When it gets strong there's no mercy."

"Don't you worry, Don Pascual. We had a scare, that's for sure, but that was all."

"Last year two French boys fell in," he said, staring at the gear spread out on the floor. "They brought all kinds of things. Even radios. They came to look at some caves. They went in over there, underneath. Then the river swelled up and whoooosh," he said, half-closing his eyes, his face creasing, a hand flitting in the air. "They never came out. My youngest grandson helped rescue one of them. He was a rag doll by then. Not even that. Just skin and ground-up bones. The ropes turned up close to the bottom, all tangled up with a rock when the river calmed down."

"French boys? I hadn't heard about that. Don't worry, though. We're not French. And we don't go down, we climb up," I said, smiling.

"Hmmph. Down, up, it's all the same. The river doesn't care. *Criollo*, gringo, it's all the same. It comes and *boom*. And they even brought radios," he concluded with another flutter of his hand. His fingernails were dense and coarse as a turtle shell, dirt-stained, his hands and fingers thick, marked by what I imagined were old farmer's wounds. Trades come to inhabit the body. His nails grew downward like an eagle's.

"I have a great-granddaughter who looks just like you, you know that? Just like you," he insisted. He centered his hat on his head, blessed me, and set out again on the path toward the forest, stepping slowly in his rope-soled sandals and his dark pants cinched at the waist with a length of rope. I kept puttering, wondering what must have happened. To the French guys. And wondering about the great-granddaughter.

Fabi had gone out for gas and the uncoupled couple was gone for good. I was itching for a walk, so I put on my boots and left the house. No radios. No cell phone. My phone lives in the car or at home. To me, going out for a two-hour walk has always meant advancing into silence, into whatever happens. If you don't, you lose the habit: you start feeling the urge to tell the others where you are, what your plans are, when you'll be back. If you'll be back. The natural human tendency is toward heat, words, shelter. It takes discipline to stop being a herd animal. Besides, you can't match your breath with your steps if you're talking on the phone.

As you ascend, it changes—the green hue and size of the leaves, the thickness of the trunks and branches, the density of the canopies. Every five hundred meters it's a different landscape. Your body, your own landscape changes, too. Your ankles, thighs, and chest are speaking to you, contracting and expanding with every step. You're muscle and then you're air inflating your belly, you're orphaned thought, shipwrecked thought, you don't think at all. Or what you think slips out of you and attaches to a tree trunk. There it stays. You're phosphorescent moss and then you're eucalyptus. You're thirst, numb feet, red skin prickling, a pulsing in your head. You're more thirst and thirst postponed. You're suspended moment. You're patience. When you descend again, you're waterfall. A foot on every rock. You're a grasshopper. You stop being everything you come to be when you talk along the way. Life goes silent when you talk.

Back at the house, I found Rafael stretched out in front of the house, sprawled out on the front lawn, a forearm slung across his forehead to block the sun, a pack beside him, and half a tangerine resting on his bare abdomen. His feet and ankles were slicked with something black that looked like petroleum. He'd fixed his perennial Hawaiian shorts with duct tape on one of the legs. I lay down beside him without a sound. We stayed there for a while. Not touching.

"How's it going?" he said after a bit.

"How was Kukenán?"

"Meh. It rained a lot. I'm beat. All the way back in one go. Twenty-two hours." After several long seconds, he added, "Tomás kept going. By bus."

Soon we were crossing the river. We reached Mars. A wall covered in craters from the base up to the anchor. A long, sustained route. I had two goals: that wall, because of its color and how perfectly carved its holes appear along the way, and Mount Roraima, because of its vertical walls, its landscape, and its female name.

That afternoon I started the route from the bottom up, without falling, on sight. Once at the anchor, with my legs spread and braced against the rock on both sides, hung with my entire weight into the harness and onto the taut rope, I loosened my shoes, bared my heels to release my toes from the pressure, and secured Rafael. When he reached me, he drew up the rope, which brought the pack along with it: the bed, the kitchen, that night's dinner, and the next day's breakfast.

"Good." And he grasped my hand in his rough, solid hands, and he gave me a hug, hard but brief.

"Bet it wouldn't have rained so much if you'd invited me to come with you," I said, skating over our brusque goodbye at La Guairita and trying to make a joke. We set up the hanging bed. From this aerial cot, rope-suspended, we looked out at the river below and its crossing points in the distance. I left my harness on. The light was dimming.

"What was I supposed to do, Bird?"

"To tell them. You say what you want and then you see, right?"

"Asparagus soup or chicken with noodles?"

"Chicken with noodles. Why didn't you tell them? Why don't you ever tell them I want to go?"

"Chicken with noodles. Because you don't come with me. You come when you're invited on your own. When you're asked as another person in the group. You don't come with me."

"Your loss."

"Maybe so. Look over there," he said, gesturing toward the snake that was the river. "This place is something else."

One of the things I liked best about traveling with Rafael was listening to his tone of voice, the volume he printed on every word. I don't think I ever heard him yell—just that one time at La Guairita, or when he fought with other people. I saw him fight twice, maybe three times. Four tops. I don't know. Not many. Even·in our worst moments I was captivated by his voice, his purring. It was like traveling with your house on your back.

I never saw Pascual again. On the way back to Caracas, passing by his house, I saw Canelo the dog tied to a tree with a pink and green climbing rope, thick and flayed. I thought it must have been the French guys' rope. That same year Tomás told me that Don Pascual had died. He went to La Puerta to rent the house, but they told him it wasn't available anymore; a great-granddaughter and her family live there now.

"Julia, you won't believe this," he told me by phone later. "The granddaughter looks just like you. Identical. You have a clone in La Puerta."

I've kept three photos of that expedition with Rafael. In one, his face peeks out, framed by the intense violet color of the hanging bed. Below, the river, the wall of blurry rock, everything else unfocused. In the next photo I'm lying on my back. We both look like we've just woken up. My whole body is visible, and my expression is surprised or even pleased, as if I'd arrived by dream and had just opened my eyes to discover myself suspended from the heights, with Rafael. In the last photo, our feet are ringed by the purple of the bed, the orange of his sleeping back, and a couple blue and green safety belts. The camera must have gone off by itself; no one took this photo. And there are our feet, blurry, unsuspecting, floating in mid-air.

We were naked in places you can't picture humans even existing. On cliffs. On rocks jutting out into gorges. In lightless caves. Underground. In the sea. And in tents on slopes, surrounded by ice, enveloped in blizzards that threatened to yank us out of the snow with a single jolt. On deserted paths, attentive to any sound that might signal the approach of someone or something. The division between public and private space, between mattress and craggy rock, was useless to us. We were in places where the only thing present apart from the two of us, and the occasional ant, was an abyss. My life depended on Rafael and on whatever he decided to do with his own. And the other way around: I held him in my hands. This is normal, just part of the deal between climbers. But to have your physical existence depend on the person who sees you naked and knows the fragility of your skin, it's a primitive thing. With every onslaught of desire, the person who causes you pleasure and watches your expression seized with it is also looking into the abyss; he is your abyss, too. You're mere millimeters from the edge, with a body on top of you that could erase you entirely. A body you could make disappear.

But my friends were his friends and they loved him. They said that if you forgot about the drinking for a minute, Rafael was the best climbing partner you could possibly have. What our friends said became a solid point in favor of the violent stories that circled Rafael like flies, but it also defended his case when I decided to trust him. If you forget about all that, he's the best partner you could have, they'd tell me.

"You know you can come wherever I go, right?"

At first I'd press play and study the panic in his face, a frightened face that can't go back, knowing he'll have to swallow the bitter taste, breathe, count, open his wings, and take a step forward. There's nothing left behind; there's nothing left. Whatever happens will happen. He waves with one hand, holding the camera in the other. He blows a kiss. The image shifts, his fingers block the lens, tremulous, ready: the camera's locked into his helmet. He says something incomprehensible in a quavery voice. You can't hide fear. You can ignore it, downplay it. But you can't hide the tremor. The video shows bits of his purple suit. The emerald glacier beneath his feet. The nervous image, shifting in and out of focus, his rapid breath. Rafael shouting. Inflating his chest to the wind, to the glacier. I don't see this part but I know it's what he's doing. He plummets closer and closer to earth until his parachute explodes and the image leaps. There's the sound of a sharp inhalation. And everything slows down. Rafael floats. At the end, the image bounces, shows him running a little, the parachute strings dropping groundward with the weight of the canopy. His hands cover the lens; he disengages the camera from the helmet. And he films himself letting out a wild yell. Another.

"A...maaaaaa...ziiiing!" he says, his voice still agitated, somewhere between shouting and sighing. I can't hear his heart but I know it's about to burst. He films the white-gray landscape all around him.

When I left on my trip, even though I had no way to watch a DVD, the disc came with me everywhere. It became an anchor. With the video on play, I'd search for some missing trace in his pupils, a sign before he hurled himself into the void. I could see the camera reflected in his right iris, seeing him back. No one behind him. The landscape. Nothing else. I felt less alone with the CD in my backpack. You always knew he'd disappear, I'd tell myself. Just like that. *Poof.* 舟

Chapter V

You take something out of your pack, anything at all—a pair of socks, say—and suddenly everything's a mess inside it. Then you try to organize your backpack and the chaos migrates to the tent. Now you can't find the socks you just set aside. You can't find your lighter. One glove emerges but not the other. By the time you find the missing glove, the one you were holding in your hand just a second ago has vanished, and in the same instant you discover half a chocolate bar you'd been searching for the previous night.

We'd headed up to the Sierra Nevada de Mérida with the plan to stay ten days or so, camp at the Laguna Verde, climb Pico Humboldt and then Pico Bolívar. On our day off, Rafael went out for a walk (so I don't get rusty, Bird) and I stayed at the camp, surrounded by *frailejones* and bushes, looking out at the glacial riverbed. I walked around the lagoon, cleaned up what was left of breakfast, tidied the tent. I washed my underwear. I lay down on my sleeping bag without bothering to zip it up.

Breathing. In a landscape like this one, you have to really open your eyes and listen to the peace. Understand what your body is asking for. Let its needs guide you. I smoked a joint under the tent's orange canopy. I imagined Rafael coming in through the doorway. I blotted the image from my mind and imagined someone else, a tousle-haired stranger, strong hands gripping my pelvic bones, stroking my pubis, searching between my legs.

I fell asleep with the final shudder.

"Bird," he said from outside, calling me back. I heard the clatter of dishes, the zip-zip of a backpack opening and closing.

"*Arepas* or four-cheese spaghetti? Bird! Are you asleep? Come out here and talk to me." He opened the tent. "I met some French climbers. One of them's looking for a partner and she looks strong. Do you want to climb Humboldt again? I feel bad for them—they seem cool, and they're as lost as the Lindbergh baby. Pasta or *arepas*?" he said, leaving my line of vision and starting to arrange the dishes near the kitchen.

"Anyway! Aren't you coming out?" he continued. "Where's the sauce? It looks like you tried to clean things up and just made another mess," he said, and ducked back into the tent.

"What about the guy? What's he going to climb?" I asked. He came closer.

"I'm talking about her. She needs a partner. He's going somewhere else," he said as I opened my arms to him. "He might come with me," he added. He got into the sleeping bag. We both pulled down his polar fleece pants and tangled our legs together.

"Not hungry?" he asked as I tugged off his sweater and everything below it. I turned toward his feet, formed a small undulating tent around his pelvis. I could half-see inside the sleeping bag. He grabbed me by the hair as I took him in my mouth and I felt smothered. He wouldn't let me come back up. I bit at his hips to shake him off and he pushed me face down, pulled open my legs. I ended up with a zipper pressed into my cheek. The water was boiling outside. I sat astride him, pushing him hard into the ground. That night he showed me the bruise on his lower back. There's nothing better than shouting on the mountain.

"Fuck! Food's burning," he said afterward, sitting up like a spring. "The duathlon left me shaking. If I don't eat right now, I'll pass out."

When I emerged, I found him circling the pot, smoking a cigarette and singing.

"Fucking Perales. What a master."

We made love gently that night. Fell into a heavy sleep.

"Anything for me?" was the first thing I'd ask whenever I got home in Caracas. The answer was usually no, accompanied by a look of reproach from my mother: "For dinner, noodle soup. As for the mail, same as yesterday."

But every so often I was met with an envelope, addressed in Rafael's incorrigibly first-grade handwriting. On those afternoons, I'd shut myself up in my room, sit on the floor, and open the letter very slowly, silent and alone. An autumn leaf, a sticker bearing the logo of some brand-name climbing or mountaineering gear, a photo of some landscape devoid of human life, a postcard with a short, affectionate phrase.

Once he sent me a napkin from Peru that said "hi bird hi bird hi bird" on both sides. Later, from Colombia, a set of animal-themed trading cards that used to come tucked into Jet chocolate packages (I think the Colombians call chocolates *chocolatinas* and playing cards *pegantinas*). We began formally collecting the cards later on, when I traveled there and met up with Rafael and Fabián, now staying in Suesca and occasionally working as Andean guides.

Sometimes the envelope contained only a drawing. I still have one that shows a mountain and an ascent line, sketched in pen, with an arrow pointing toward the place where a stick figure says in a speech bubble: "*¡Aguanile!* Dancing on the summit of Chopicalqui!" The letters were rarely written as letters. Instead, they talked about peaks and altitudes, new plans, climbing teams taking shape. A gig in Huaraz as a guide, the management of a mountain shelter near Chimborazo, a slide projection in a Barcelona hiking center.

At first, I'd celebrate the arrival of these letters and the stories they told, and I'd spread the message in La Guairita; I was a sort of messenger, a privileged liaison between Rafael and everyone else. I'd save certain details for Lupe. At school, I'd tell María Auxiliadora, who didn't really understand. But after a particular point, when the sex and the tightrope walks and the ropeless ascents and the wall-beds and the stoves lit in subzero temperatures had started to accumulate, I began to muffle what little I knew. I stopped sharing news and announcing plans or changes-of-plans. People would ask and I'd say I had no idea. Once his mother called me and I did the same thing: "I have no idea," I told her. "I haven't heard anything. Of course, if I get any news, I'll let you know," I added before I hung up, fiddling with the postcard that said he was in Chile and coming back in two weeks. You know the drill, he'd written in a corner at the end. Call my mom and tell her I'm OK.

Not so tough now, are you? Call her yourself. So I'm a secretary, huh. I'm just your secretary or what. Call her yourself.

But I'd keep asking the same questions each time I came home. By now, the wait made me sad, but I didn't run away or complain. That was the beginning of it all: learning the uselessness of asking for more. It was all about discipline at first. And then it was pride: when you ask and someone gives you what you'd asked for, you don't know whether he did it as a favor or because he really wanted you to have it. And what do you gain from that? Silence is better. Which is why I started out by asking him to tell me about his plans and reporting them to the others, but eventually I stopped asking and stopped sharing what I learned.

In the end, I stopped finding things out altogether. It was easier that way. If the person doesn't tell you anything, then you don't have to tell anything, either. Sometimes silence is safer, freer. If you don't ask, then no one asks you. In the end, I needed to know he was okay more than I needed to know whose sleeping bag he was zipping into his at night, or who was with him on his days off. Regardless, the style of a note, the length of a phone call, the amount of time he'd been off the grid—all of this said a lot. I learned to read him. And I guess he learned to read me, too. We felt our way into a wordless pact.

Rafael had his own list of suspicions and unasked questions, as I'd learn later.

I'd keep waiting for his letters and I'd celebrate their arrival with my ritual. Sitting on the floor, in the same corner of my bedroom, alone. But the thing is, goddammit, that when an incredible climb, a phenomenal fuck, and two months of silence are punctuated by a chocolate bar wrapper, a sticker, and a stupid drawing on a napkin—I mean, that's shameless. ⌗

CHAPTER VI

We traveled by bus to the Sierra Nevada del Cocuy. I made brownies.

"Now this is classy. This is the good shit. It's like lava," he'd say with every bite, licking his fingers, his teeth smeared with chocolate. He had a six-pack of beer in his backpack. Always cans. Firm believers in symbolic power, we never bought anything bottled. It was a short trip, and it wasn't like the duration really mattered, but we were well equipped, so the time flew. The bus made two stops. We got off together the first time, stretched our legs, went to pee.

At the second stop, he got off alone. I watched him through the window, half-asleep. He walked toward the truckers' parking lot and continued all the way to the highway. He left the restrooms and the soda fountain behind. One of the advantages of being a man, I thought. Not just having a dick and getting to piss standing up, but also not fearing the border when you stand between a gas station and the open road at two-thirty in the morning, trusting that you can afford to lower your pants and pee in the grass instead of going into the restrooms, which are always disgusting. Before we'd left his place, I'd made him swear.

"Relax," he'd said. "I know how it is. The border's full of sketchy people. I'll behave."

Rafael dropped his pants. When he was done, he pulled them up again. And he didn't come back. He stayed on the traffic island, looking from side to side. Presiding. Hands in his pockets like someone waiting. I could have sworn he was whistling. He took something out of his pocket and lit it.

Goddammit, Rafael. You promised.

He began to shift the firefly from one hand to the other, as if he were on a rock shelf in the middle of La Gran Sabana. It was very cold inside the bus. The other passengers, except for a mother nursing her child and a guy near the door with headphones on, had gotten out and slipped into one of three lines: one for the bathroom; one to buy empanadas, pastries, candy, or *guayoyo* coffee from the soda fountain; and one to talk on a rented cell phone administered by a plump woman who was sitting on a soda crate behind a plastic table. Her ass must always be waffle-stamped by the end of her shift. I got off the bus and waited in line for the restroom. From outside, the floor looked partly plastered with brown blotting paper. I could see Rafael in the distance, floating in his bubble of smoke.

As I waited, I wondered which were worse, Colombian cops or Venezuelan cops. If they nab you smoking weed in a place like this, which would be more dangerous. Then I wondered where they'd take you—to a cell in which country. It smelled like shit around me, which wasn't so bad. If it smells like shit, it's because the smell of marijuana doesn't reach where you are. I went into the bathroom stall without touching anything, peed, and didn't even try to flush. At the sink, I found nothing but the trace of an old flood, an already dried-out green-gray horizontal line. The soap dispenser looked rusted over and was coated with blobs of pink gel. There was no water, and the shortage was announced on a sheet of paper stuck to the mirror, which concluded, after breaking the news, with "SO DONT MAKE A MESS THANKYOU." I walked back out toward the gas station with a sense of reinforced repulsion, navigating the brown puddles toward the highway.

We sat on the curb of the traffic island. Trucks clamored by. Six or seven semi-trailer trucks parked in front of us. We could make out the drivers' hammocks hung between the wheels of three of them. Blackened by soot and oil. They nearly touched the ground and looked deformed with weight. Rafael passed me the pipe. I didn't feel like smoking, but I took it. This happens to me sometimes—I don't want to smoke but I smoke anyway. I wasn't afraid anymore. On the other side, three scantily dressed, thick-legged women chatted with two drivers of a Polar truck; they seemed to know each other. A bus drove by very fast, honking. The gust of wind made me shiver.

"Shit. A *borrador*. An eraser. "

They're not nicknamed *borradores* for nothing. "Erasers." The buses that take you to Choroní drive at a breakneck pace, snaking their way along the curves of the mountain road. A narrow path traversed by rivers that appear and disappear with the seasons, and sometimes by fallen trees—casualties of the tropical forest humidity. The buses go at top speed, honking like crazy, never braking. If you don't get out of their way—well, you get erased. Like scrap metal, plunging into the void. I've seen at least five cars forced off the edge of a cliff by a *borrador*. You pass them, looking down on them from above, from the road, where the ambulances, fire trucks, and stretchers take their time to show up and try to rescue the accident victims down below. You're partially responsible for what the *borrador*-driver does to others. No one complains. When you make it to the beach, you smoke your first joint, drink your first beer, get into the water, and everything stays there.

When I looked back to the group of passengers we'd come with, only three people were still outside. We walked toward the bus. Shared a piece of gum.

"We should go to Choroní."

I said nothing.

"Let's go. Don't you want to? We'll dance to the drums and relax on the beach."

"Do you really think I'd still want to?" I answered.

He turned toward the road. "It's the same old story with you," he said, frustrated. "The fight with that German guy was just shitty luck, Bird. I've already said that a million times. Come on. I'll take you. And no *guarapita*. I promise you I won't drink any *guarapita*."

"It'd take a miracle for you to keep a promise."

"I swear. I mean it."

We got back onto the bus. I fell asleep as soon as we'd left the gas bumps behind. I woke up somewhere along the way, freezing.

"Hang in there. We've got four hours to go," he said. "The cold doesn't exist."

Rafael covered me with a wine-colored plane blanket. He passed me a water bottle I hadn't asked for, despite my heavy tongue and thick saliva. He took out a can of beer and polished it off in three swigs. Left the can on the floor. I shifted my arms under the blanket and curled up, soothed by the pleasant announcement of heat. I felt a hand—he pulled me toward him by the leg, unbuttoned my jeans. I glanced around us. My lids leaden, prickling. It was dark. Four small TV sets displayed a soap commercial on mute: two women comparing garments they'd just pulled out of the washing machine. One looked crestfallen as she held up a still-soiled shirt and regarded the lily white one in the other's hands. A celestial man appeared and seemed to lecture the loser about the results obtained by the second woman, who smiled proudly.

I closed my eyes. Rafael offered me a half-chewed mouthful of brownie. In a few more days, I'll reach the summit of Ritacuba Blanco, travel to Suesca, and stay three weeks longer than planned. I'll balance my way along the train tracks with my eyes shut. I'll be told that the train never comes, but one day I'll feel it thrumming under my feet, and as I got off the tracks to wait, I'll feel the breeze on my face as it rushes past. I'll take photos of the meadow and the tracks. Years later, I'll be stunned by the beauty of a yellow light I never noticed at the time. I'll catwalk my way across the tightrope connecting two trees. I'll confirm that when the ground is far away, it's difficult to keep your balance on the rope; you lose all sense of horizontality and you struggle harder. I'll smoke a lot and eat Twinkies and baked plantains with cheese and *bocadillos*. I'll watch Rafael fuck another woman. I won't say a word. I'll collect playing cards in packages of Jet chocolate. My clothes will be tight on me when I get home. I'll make the return trip alone.

But now I was on the bus, with my eyes closed, where the TV screens and the aisle lights went off moments later. The taste of brownies. The only noise came from the wind banging against the window fittings, the whistle of it, and the swish of wheels over pavement. Behind my eyelids, the highway glimmers approaching head-on. I curled up over his legs, unzipped his pants. The memory of the sweet taste in my mouth ceded to the sweat of his balls, the liquid forewarnings of his stiff cock. His hands slipped confidently under my blanket and between my legs. Please, let the seat-back stay still, let the seat be silent. Let the violent submission end in a pair of sighs. Outside, the wind blew toward the eraser we were. More tingling under my eyelids, more longing to sleep.

We brought both the rock and ice gear this time. I was carrying over fifty pounds in food and equipment. Fabián and Rafael each had a backpack exceeding them in height by a couple heads and which couldn't have weighed much less than ninety pounds. The packs rose up a foot above their skulls. They were about to burst.

You're supposed to transport up to a third of your body weight, but each of us was carrying more than half on our backs. And you feel it—your knees pop. Rusty hinges. People say that it gets worse with age; you crack all the time. When you stoop down. When you stretch more than usual. A clock. A second-hand. Everything's on its way to an end. But you don't think about that. You can't. You wouldn't do a thing if you did. If something ends in your twenties, it's out of the blue.

Little by little, you learn to walk with those extra pounds, that annexed matter. You have to get used to the torso's movement from side to side. It's no joke; you lose your balance. When you lift one leg, you feel like all the weight shifts onto the other side, like you'll keel over. Little by little, too, your body fat starts to toughen. You touch your legs and they feel like trunnels. Inside. Outside. The last time I went to the doctor, the nurse couldn't get her head around it: she took my pulse and then my blood pressure and asked me several times if I felt all right. She looked at me suspiciously.

"Are you sure you're feeling okay? Let me know if you feel faint."

"That's just how my heart is. Slow."

"Did you have breakfast?"

We met up with Fabi in Colombia. The two of them climbed the vertical wall at Ritacuba Blanco first, all rock and ice, and then the three of us went up one of its snowy walls. There were no matchboxes or equipment to deal with. Rafael and I made our way together. Fabi walked alone because he wanted a calm trip, or so he said; he wanted to take it easy. No one said anything about Patagonia. We had to leave him alone.

During that trip, I learned that you should keep your boots inside the tent, because they'll freeze if leave them outside. Even so, putting them on in the morning is always torture. You don't put them on inside the tent so the crampons won't rip the floor, and your fingers freeze even in the short time it takes to stick your feet out toward the snow in the early morning and adjust the twenty metal holes and hooks on each plastic boot. They hurt, your fingers. Better put, you know they hurt, but you don't feel the pain. That's how the day starts: numb fingers and the silhouette of the mountain before you. Black on black. Stars. The job to be done. There are no questions at that time of day. There are rituals: every step and every item in the same order every time. After an hour or two of walking on autopilot, a strip of color appears: first red, then orange. Then the sun. Going up is a slog, coming down is a slog, and in between you have the instant of achievement, which you celebrate once you're down below again, once you're back where it all began, inside your tent. That's the thing: you return to where it all began, but you're not the same. You're another version of yourself. A better version, drained, drugged with all the cold and sweat. Happier, too.

I learned that preparing instant meals at an altitude of four thousand meters isn't as easy as the instructions on the package say it is, and that every mouthful is a luxury in those conditions. Rice is always risotto and pasta is always purée. But it's haute cuisine. You might like it or you might not, but no matter what, once you're all the way up there, at four thousand meters, everything is high-level gourmet.

I learned that you have to choose your ice carefully. You make a hole in the farthest area from the campsite, fill the pot with snow, and put it on the fire. You add salt, because if you don't you'll get insanely dehydrated. You're standing on a mass of water you can't properly drink from. It's like having a mother, but a dead one.

I also learned that granola and raw cane sugar save the day. And that the cold makes me sad. I discovered that I like beer—not because we drank it, but because of how often I imagined opening one. Breathing is the hardest part. You wake up in the middle of the night, gasping for air, heaving like a fish. As you walk and breathe in that dense, rough air, you think compulsively about the first thing you'll do once you're off the mountain: eat a pizza, have a beer, scarf down some chocolate ice cream.

To withstand the cold, you sacrifice your sense of touch. You sheathe your hands in very thin gloves, then polar fleece gloves, then thicker weatherproof gloves. So you have to look at what you're doing to know what you're doing. Grabbing the rope is a whole odyssey. Same with your feet. It's hard to know what's in contact with the snow. Above it—or below it, actually, on the soles of your feet—are the crampons, the claws you entrust to keep you from plunging off the mountain or into a ravine. The four layers of clothing, from your underwear to your raincoat, turn the body into a closet. Sunglasses, sunblock, attack backpack, harness.

I didn't understand the most important part until later. Happiness is like grass. When it's there, you don't pay any attention to it; you don't see it at all. We were silent as tears of wonder. Animals of pure, clear consciousness. Up there. On the mountain.

You're happy and don't realize it. Which is what photos are good for. To study your own eyes, remember the white hills, the canopy of a thousand pine trees under your feet, a river. In the photos, weeks later, you see your own smile as if it belonged to someone else. You revisit the texture of your hair and your dirty, greasy clothes, the feeling of your body dropping onto your sleeping bag after a ten-, twelve-hour leg; the pleasure of taking that first bite into a sweet *bocadillo*. Happiness is deceptive. More efficient backwards. It's all there in the photos.

Once you're back, you spend a week or so at a slow vibrate. Everything flows differently. You feel like you're someone else. You've come from a perfect place. You've come from looking at your body, feeling thirsty, crying for a good reason—hunger, cold, fear—and you can see all the threads in the cloth. Thanks to the mountain, you're able to make out the mechanisms that dictate daily life, life on land. You come back different.

Now that your battery has been recharged, now that you've attained this ultraviolet vision, you carry on until you need to plug back into the mountain again. Until everything starts to lose its luster. Traps appear: you need more money, you meet a guy you like, you long to have your own apartment and live like a normal person. That's the trap. If you fall in, you're fucked. You know you can't commit. So you don't look for the job you could look for. You avoid the guy who hits on you and tell him offhandedly that you have a boyfriend so he won't wait around. You know you can't afford that sort of luxury—or that you can only afford something totally different. You start to fade out, tamp yourself down. You're no one. That's where the discipline comes in. You have to erase yourself if you're going to exist. To stay alert. Resist. One day in La Guairita you start to get tired of the same routes, the same traverse, the same joint at the end. Lupe going on about her boyfriends, you giving her advice you wouldn't want to receive. You come home and find your mother picking fights with you about everything.

Okay.

Time to go away again. To recharge. To wipe your vision clean.

Rafael has a short fuse. When normalcy overwhelms him, he starts getting into brawls; he vanishes at night; he has too much energy. He has to leave. He has to leave all the time. If he didn't escape, he'd go crazy. And if I didn't escape, I'd get sad.

Sometimes, when you're traveling, you suddenly feel like sitting down on a rock and not moving for ages. They call it *anan-*

da. You stay there, staring at a pebble, a beetle, a frosty glimmer on the ground, and you want to live inside that beauty. Goodbye.

But I didn't stay on the Ritacuba. The crowning moment was a brief, mechanical event, a procedure barely seasoned by the snapping of two photos I never saw, three sips of water, and the rush to make it back down. The wind was blowing hard and a leaden stain in the clouds approached with the cold.

"Better hurry. We'll celebrate down below."

No one said a word until we reached the campsite. Silence is also an antidote to fear, a plot against dark times. Every once in a while it's good to believe that what isn't named doesn't exist. We had asparagus soup and pasta with mushrooms and parmesan cheese for dinner. Fabián brought out some Pirulín candies. We revved up the jukebox with what the CD label described as "Mountain Hits of Yesterday, Today, and Always."

"Good shit," Fabi said, wildly stoned that night, singing along: "*Chévere chévere chévere chévere chévere, oooo!*"

"Fucking classy, man. El Puma is a fucking king."

And all three of us laughed.

We laughed and sang until Rafael suddenly grew very serious. "Dude, what I mean is that if they're saying this stuff it's for a reason. You're strong. I think you should go."

"Yeah, man. That's what I'm saying," Fabi answered, biting his fingernails, his eyes huge, struggling to extract some little shard of rebellious nail. "I think I have to."

"Of course it's scary. I don't know. You're the one who knows if you're strong."

"Yeah," said Fabi, concentrating on his nails, his dry cuticles. He still hadn't looked at Rafael.

"I see a strong dude."

"Mm-hmm."

After a while, I began to feel like I was traveling alone. I was getting stronger and stronger, and I liked the silence more and more. I discovered that nothing stayed steady in our family and I learned both to adapt to the fluctuations and to ask for them. Elastic. The three of us would often sleep in the same tent, but the sleeping bags that spoke to each other were mine and Rafael's. We could attach them by linking up the zippers. We were lucky that way. I could tell that Fabi watched us some nights. He had to, no matter how silent we were: hands undressing ourselves and seeking each other, hips shifting, bodies trembling, sighs. You don't hold it in for later. What if there is no later? People say that everything extreme goes together: the desire for sex, for heights, for violence. Pain is pleasure, they say. The gringos used to say *No pain, no gain*. Now they say *No pain, no pain*. There's nothing like the old school.

You have to be able to tell them apart. The good cramps from the bad. Astonishment from suffocation. The rusty bands from the broken. The body expresses itself however it can. The law is simple: you have to feel something. If you don't, you're wasting your time. But all it takes is a missing pulse for the trip to end: a snapped anterior cruciate ligament, tendinitis of the fingers, corneal flash burns. Frostbite. Explosion against the earth.

That's the end of that.

Sometimes I'd get into the tent or come back from a walk or from washing the cooking pots in the river and I'd find them talking furtively, concluding their conversations with gestures, raising their eyebrows when I arrived. I found out about Laura from Laura herself. She'd drool all over him. She'd wiggle her ass in his face. Her eyes squinched up when Rafael appeared. I understood the whole story in spite of Caboose, who accidentally let it slip as he cleaned some weed after a traverse. I'd just gotten back from Colombia.

"Laura called. They're out in Suesca."

"Laura called?"

"Yeah. She hurt herself."

"Ah."

"Suesca's brutal."

"Poor thing. Is it bad?" I answered, just to see what else he would say.

"Pretty bad. Tennis elbow. They're going back to the Sierra because her arms can't take it." Then he went quiet and turned to look at me, setting the weed aside: "Fuck. Julia. I'm sorry, princess." He got to his feet, glanced skyward, covered his face with his hands, and let out a sigh, or more like a groan. "I'm such an idiot." He turned to face me. "Princess? Look, Julia. I'm sorry to ask this, but please don't say anything to Rafa. Be careful. He'd fuck me up. Don't tell Rafa I told you. I'm serious. He'd fucking destroy me."

"Don't worry. It's okay. But tell me everything. What's going on?'

When they came back, Laura greeted me as if nothing had happened. We climbed together. One day I asked her about Colombia and she said she'd never gone. The bitch. She climbed in a push-up bra.

You can always sense these things. Everyone knows that.

Our family had substitutions, protocols. The team would disintegrate in Caracas. Everyone had their own plans, and that was part of our plan: till next time. We'd meet up, we'd run into each other, we'd act just like we always had, and at the same time it would all be different. I had responsibilities. I was accountable to the university, to my mother. Studying and working at school had its advantages: long breaks, for example. In the summer and the winter. And then other gaps: Carnaval, Easter. The occasional student strike.

"In the clouds," my mom would tell me. "You have your head in the clouds. Why don't you look for a normal job, hon? No, of course you don't—if you got a normal job, then you wouldn't be able to run after that bum every time he decides he's in the mood to see you. But when he ignores you, then you come running right back. To finish school, you say. How do I know you didn't get expelled and you're just hiding it from me?"

"Mom, I'm on break."

"Mm-hmm. So that's what they call it these days. I bet they kicked you out."

Back home, I'd find other friends. People willing to be part of my life despite my disappearing acts, people who'd appear with a single call, a single gesture. There was María Auxiliadora; there was Lupe. Armando, who had a house, with a bed and a kitchen and a dog. He was only a weekend climber.

"No one's perfect," I'd tell him, laughing, when he'd complain about going two weeks without a climb.

We understood each other. Or at least we spoke the same language. He worked in human rights and ran marathons. He wanted a normal relationship, children.

"Julia, don't run away on me," he said the last time we saw each other, not long before what happened to my mom.

"No, I mean, look. I don't run away. It's just that life gets complicated."

It was like with Lupe and Caboose. They had a thing once. They kissed and did who knows what else in some dark corner of La Guairita. I found them out when I saw them coming down together, hand in hand, and she was floating, her cheeks aflame, suspended in the glow of momentary romance. She talked all week about the date they'd planned for Friday. I found it all very strange: at the end of the day, Caboose was Caboose and she was herself. We'd taken a thousand trips together and no one had ever noticed a thing.

But Lupe was counting the days and celebrating the plan: "First we're going to the movies and then we'll go for ice cream. No, I don't know what we're going to see."

That Friday, we all climbed together, but they barely looked at each other. Not a word between them. Before five, they gathered their stuff and left. He dropped his backpack three times on the way to the parking lot. At one point she tripped on her own foot and nearly fell. She called me several times to ask what I thought she would wear, what to do if Caboose asked her over to his place, because wasn't it kind of soon, she wasn't sure if she should sleep with him or not. On the last call, she assured me she wouldn't fuck him in the car: "Not like *that*," she said.

That was it.

On Saturday, Lupe wouldn't look me in the eye. She hardly spoke to me during several routes, and before she went off to a solo traverse, she said: "Juli. Caboose looks so weird when he dresses like a normal person. He's like a preppy teenager. His pants cinched at the waist, groomed from head to toe. He wears a belt." She sounded offended: "He looks so bland."

"You want to want him, but you don't," I told her. "Relax. There's nothing you can do about it."

"It's just that he looks so weird in real clothes. His jeans are kind of tight on him and he wears moccasins with no socks."

You'd get used to seeing them shirtless, with their even tans and the abs that emerge when you're not paying attention and have no say in the matter, after months of climbing walls all day long. Their soil-streaked shorts, their bare, callused feet. Climbers forget how to wear clothes, and then other people can spot the novelty of it in us. Poor Lupe. And poor Caboose, who ended up lovesick without even understanding what had happened.

"I don't get it—what did I do? I call and she doesn't answer, and if someone else picks up, they won't hand her the phone. They always have some excuse."

And what was I supposed to say to him? It's the moccasins, Caboose. It's all about the moccasins. Take off your shirt. Get dirty.

It's not easy to feel attracted to a normal guy. Armando, for example. Not easy. The same thing happened to me with him. Later I ended up bending over backwards, trying to patch things up, and by then it was too late. But whatever. It's not a big deal. So it goes.

"From now on, Caboose," I told him months later, when we were all drunk, "golden rule. From now on. Pay attention, okay, because I know what I'm talking about. No moccasins. Roll up your cuffs. Let's see. Definitely not without socks," I said, concluding my inspection.

That was around the time I started planning Salto Ángel. I got a topographical map and began to study the route. I imagined myself looking up from the river, immersed in the mist at the base of the waterfall, feeling the droplets like dew on my face. I dreamed about it. I randomly found a little piece of jasper and carried it in my pocket everywhere. The walls look huge from down below. When you stand up and look toward the top, you grasp what a thousand meters really means, with its stains of color and its overhangs and its caves, its shelves. Armando got a job in Mexico City sometime around then. I found out by mail. A postcard that was somewhat different from the others. A well-written postcard, no spelling errors, with decent handwriting, expressing actual feelings. That he'd left without saying goodbye because he guessed I probably wasn't in Caracas. That you'll always be successful and good luck with everything you strive for. I'm here in Mexico if ever need anything. I live near a cold, pretty park in the middle of the city. I go there to run every day.

"You choose your own cross to bear. You like it when they leave you," my mother declared when she found the postcard I hadn't put away. Maybe I'd left it out on purpose, maybe I wanted her to know: "No more Armando, Mom. What's done is done."

I didn't write him back. He disappeared. When Salto Ángel was finally approaching, Rafael started to talk about how ace it would be to jump off.

"Can you imagine? Climbing up together and me flying back down? They say it's the best flight there is."

When I didn't respond, he applied another strategy: "The dangerous part isn't having an accident, Bird. Look what came out in the last issue of *Climbing*, just like I'm always telling you: the tricky part is how to use the ropes during the rescue. Not everyone knows how to set up a rappel like this one. Collateral accidents, that's what the magazine calls them. Imagine this: you go, you go splat, and then the guy who's supposed to rescue you fucks up and instead of getting you out, he throws you back in. Thriller. Black and Decker. Collateral accidents. That's what they're called."

This is how he'd say it, looking elsewhere, as if he'd gotten distracted.

"When Emiliano's girlfriend left him," he said once, "the guy went up Humbolt in a rage without telling anyone. They found him four days later. He was like a human ice cube. He'd broken his femur, they said. The bitch cried then. She cried like an idiot then, that's for sure. Then they said that she'd been writing him for three days: 'Ohhhh, I forgive you, Emiliano.' Idiot. A broken femur means as good as dead. Collateral accidents. Am I right?"

"This is different."

"Okay, okay, Bird. It's true. Just an example."

When he saw that I wasn't falling for his hints, he went for the lowest blow. That's what I told him when he said, "It would be amazing to go to sleep on that wall. You and me."

"I'd love to, Rafael," I told him at last. "Next time. Who knows. If it happens, it happens. Whatever happens, happens," I concluded, withholding the pleasure of saying no. 舌

CHAPTER VII

You can't know what you'll do when faced with a thousand-meter wall until you beat it. And you don't get where you've gotten overnight. It's a slog. Then you look yourself in the eye. No mirror, no one passing judgment. When you're standing in front of a dumpster, that's when you find out whether you'll end up eating out of it. When you're offered the job, that's when you find out whether you'll end up smuggling tabs of LSD through customs in a notebook. When your best friend's boyfriend hits on you, that's when you find out whether you're capable of sleeping with your best friend's boyfriend. When you have a diploma in your hand, that's when you find out whether you'll end up spending sleepless nights surrounded by four walls, scaling the pyramid of articles and conferences after you get your Ph.D. The rest is bullshit. All talk.

People compress. Oblige. Restrict. Words are confusing. You don't know who you're going to be until you get out of the ecosystem that makes you be one thing or another. You don't know what you're capable of until you're not there anymore. Carabiner in hand. Tied into the harness. One day you find yourself climbing ropeless. It's a step. No need to plan it. It's a moment. You decide to untie yourself and place one foot, grip with one hand. And you start to climb. Two more meters. Three. It's easy. When you start out, you don't even look down. One instant, you're here; the next, you're in a limbo that can only end at the top. You can't stay halfway up that wall.

It's the same thing. You don't know what you'll do with a tight-rope on the edge of a precipice until you find yourself there. One instant, you're facing the chasm; the next, you're lifting your foot onto the rope. You step away from the edge and start walking into the air. You can't just change your mind or stay in the void forever.

Sometimes the abyss intimidates you. One blow to the spine and that's it: you're in a wheelchair or on crutches for the rest of your life. And what are you without a body? What are you without a mind? These risks are part of the deal. No New Age bullshit is worth it in the end. "We're not our bodies," blah blah blah. Of course we're our bodies! It's part of the deal, that's all. You have to watch out.

Alejo never recovered fragments of his past. He remembered his girlfriend, his relatives, the steps of the traverse, and how to manage the equipment. But the trips, part of his childhood and college years, his less-constant friends—we were all erased from his memory, and we had to rebuild the friendship from scratch. Alejo forgot his penchants and his problems. He discovered chocolate ice cream at the age of thirty-two. He was an alien who'd just landed on Earth. He ate a pint of ice cream every day.

"You never know. What if I forget this incredible stuff all over again? You gotta seize the day."

He lived in fear of continuing to forget, even though everyone told him he wouldn't, that however little or however much was left in his damaged head couldn't be blotted out again. I mention the ice cream incident because I saw it happen, but there must have been far more important labyrinths and disappearances in his mind. I can't be sure, but I bet it's true.

"Have we climbed together?" he asked me at the entrance to a cave along the traverse. "Weird, right?" He came a little closer. Proud chest, peacocking. "What about the other thing?" he asked, pressing me into the wall. "If you give me a chance, I won't waste time. I won't let you off the hook."

When we heard the others' voices, I slipped out from under his arms, drawing in my neck like a turtle. I continued my traverse. He stayed to talk with the rest. He never said another word or asked me about the two of us.

Returning unscathed is as good as never going anywhere. You have to come back with at least one real risk behind you, with a prize. Something lost or given away. You have to feel and change something. You can't be the same person once you're back. Or maybe that's just what I tell myself now, to console myself.

Traveling with tourists is totally different. You're not a climber then. No one cares that you're a climber. They want you to be a cook, a nanny, a therapist. Suddenly you find yourself in the middle of arguments between mothers and daughters, partners or spouses, best friends or former best friends, who will inexplicably start to stare daggers at each other and explode at the end of a very long or very cold day. You're the one who knows they're just exhausted.

You often feel like screaming in their faces. Like telling the mom to leave her daughter alone, that nothing bad will happen to the little shit if she takes a walk by herself. Listening to the woman who constantly picks fights with her boyfriend, you feel like telling her yes, it's true, the guy has indeed been looking at my ass all day, but that's not all; I've seen him looking at all the other women's asses, too. You're right. Leave the moron and live your life, you want to tell the girl. Better to take the bull by the horns.

The days are long. People's knees hurt and their brains stop working. They get sad. Who are you without your body? Who are you without your mind? They're connected. One of them shuts down and the other one collapses behind it. The trip grows unbearable and someone always pays the price. The guide, for example. The demons emerge. For the good of the excursion, it's your job to learn all the details, silence your opinions, and become a justice of the peace. Become a magician, a singer, a clown. You find out what you don't want to know. But work is work and you'll do anything to distract the tourists. You have to fix things. There's no point in getting dramatic, because either way, sooner or later, ta-da!, endorphins to the rescue: everyone's happy when it's over. You eat three times a day, you take things slow, you stop more along the way. You talk more. Walking so slowly makes you even more tired. The more hours on foot, the more wear-and-tear. Speed is a luxury. If you go fast, you'll have energy everywhere you go. But work is work and when it's time for the grind, it's time for the grind.

When you go on your own, you're royalty. The prize is the peak you've summited, the certainty that you've controlled yourself, stayed focused. Who gives a shit about moving trains. You're a grain of sand, you're a tiny part of this huge whole, you tell yourself. You eat whatever; you sleep wherever as long as you get to keep moving. I've seen Rafael pick up scraps of food from the ground or garbage cans in public places, nab abandoned pizzas or half-full cups of soft drinks from soda fountains in parks or nature preserves. After hours of walking, multiple joints, and with no food in your belly, there's no shame left. But the body is unforgiving.

"So our plans don't shit all over us," he told me, holding out a little white pill on the day we commenced the biannual practice I still uphold. Better to act before the cramps, diarrhea, and cold sweats sneak up on you in the worst possible place, right when you least expect them.

As far as I know, I haven't eaten from the trash, but I've certainly eaten badly cooked or possibly expired meals, remnants from other people's expeditions, and mammals I never imagined were suitable for eating. I've gone hungry, spent days ingesting nothing but water and chocolate or bread and oatmeal. We ate a mono-diet on several occasions. There was one trip to Mérida when bad weather meant we did nothing but fuck and sleep. We were left with fewer and fewer provisions as we waited for the sky to clear. In the end, we spent three days eating only salami, condensed milk, and María cookies. Food is overrated; people eat all day long. On the way back from Kukenán, I fell on a rappel and we had to take a detour, searching for an emergency clinic in a nameless tropical hole. That's where I got the hypertrophic scar on my shoulder, a slender rope embedded in my skin to remember it all. When I fell, we weren't carrying any food and we didn't eat until eighteen hours later. Watery coffee and some *acemita* bread. Two years prior, he'd had an accident in the same area, in the middle of the jungle, and he had to patch the wound with duct tape. With his leg bound up in this makeshift way, he walked for eleven hours without eating and managed to keep from bleeding to death until he reached Santa Elena de Uairén: the same medical center in the middle of nowhere where they later stitched me up, too.

"Don't worry, little lady. Getting smashed up more than once in the same spot has to be worth something. Mine was fucked up, though—we really didn't have a fucking clue where to go."

When I met Rafael, he was training with ankle weights, going up and down the stairs of his building. Fifteen floors. Ten reps of four buildings. Despite those forty times a day from the ground floor to the fifteenth, increasing the burden over time, his legs stayed as skinny as bamboo. I never understood why it wasn't enough for him to know he was strong; he also wanted to look the part. To look big. He'd make these smoothies with banana, cow's eye, sometimes raw egg.

"It's gasoline. I'll make you one sometime. They taste good with malt. If you add malt, you don't even notice the eye."

"Over my dead body."

It turns out that if you weigh an extra pound, you have to lift an extra pound into the air. It sounds obvious, but it's not. You learn it as you go. It's a strange equation: the skinnier, the stronger. And the freer you are to carry the equipment you want. Nuts, a pair of boots for every climb, straps, ropes, food: everything weighs something. You can bring what you need on a climbing rack slung across your chest. As long as you can carry it, that is. If you can't, you're screwed. And if you're fat as a balloon, you can't handle yourself or anyone else. You have to be thin; your bones have to show. The muscles develop by themselves. They just do.

"So what happened to the bones you used to have here?" he asked once, touching me on the lower back after fucking. It was cold. He was still behind me; my eyes were fixed on the orange of the tent. I sat down. I kept my back to him as I pulled on my shirt. My Lycra pants, too. I dressed under the sleeping back. I emerged fully clothed from the chrysalis. Embarrassed. I grabbed my Boreal boots and the chalk bag. A water bottle outside the tent. An orange. It was dark by the time I returned and I slipped straight into the sleeping bag. I woke with my hands dirty and aching, hungry. Dizzy with hunger. What you don't realize is that your period stops if you don't eat. During the first and second months, I spent nights wondering how to tell him I was pregnant, wondering what to do. I couldn't sleep and couldn't figure it out. I couldn't bring myself to buy a pregnancy test; I'd walk past the pharmacy and never go in. I imagined myself raising my child in some mountain village—I don't know what came over me with the farming idea, but I always found myself turning back to it when things got bad. I imagined myself planting tubers or strawberries, living in a shack in the Andes. I saw myself happy amid an unhappy outcome. Rafael appearing sporadically, accompanied by childless women and other men I'd cook for, offer clay mugs of coffee strained in a cone-shaped cloth filter. I saw myself calm.

"Don't you worry; I'll knock you up when it's time," he said when I gathered up the courage to tell him, because my period simply wouldn't come, and I'd started worrying not about his child, abandoned before gestation, but about my fertility. "My feelings are too strong for you, princess. I could stop a moving train. Don't you worry."

At a certain point, I got honest with myself. I didn't want to have a child. Or at least not with Rafael. I learned to manage my cycles, to eat almost nothing. To discipline myself. And that's what I did. At first it was all good news: I wouldn't have to travel with pads or tampons, wouldn't run out in the middle of a trip. I stopped fretting over stained clothes during long hikes, red smears in my sleep sack, the cloying, acidic scent of sex and blood. Free at last. I didn't have to deal with bags and waste: that smell of sweaty plastic and dried blood vanished from my supplies. As a woman, I started to enjoy men's liberties. Imagine climbing a mountain with cramps, undressing along the trail when you have to change your pads or tampons, when it's cold and you've got all those layers of clothes on, or inside the tent in the company of two or three other people. Sometimes women have to be men if we're going to prove what women can do. I guess my mom would say something like that. ◫

CHAPTER VIII

I've always camped furtively in Yosemite—on rock slabs, surrounded by boulders and pines, by invisible Grizzly bears I know
are within close range, and by park rangers, who are just as dangerous as the colossal animals I'm so curious about. Every night,
you roll out the sleeping mats and pull the sleeping bags from
their compression sacks. Before you crawl in, you push your shoes,
headlamps, and water bottles all the way to the bottom. If you get
thirsty in the middle of the night, you shrink up like an accordion and reach for the bottle with your feet. Same thing if you need
to pee: you curl up and find your shoes. The sleeping bag is your
bedroom, the only place where scorpions and cockroaches supposedly can't find their way in. Every morning, you follow the pro-
cess in reverse until you're holding the down bag and the rolled-up
sleeping mats in each hand. You clear your campsite, leaving no
trace of the overnight stay you didn't pay a cent for. Before my second trip to the park, I bought the Wizard of Oz. It cost me three
hundred dollars and it took us everywhere, slow but steady.

"What do you mean, *wizard*? This is a piece of junk," he said
when I pulled up alongside him.

"It cost as much as a jacket."

"It'll break down as soon as you hit the highway. You'll see."

"What you want is to know where I am and where I'm going,"
I said, jabbing my index finger against the palm of my other hand.
"You like having me here."

"I don't understand why we need two cars. We already have Fabi's."

In the mornings, we'd store our gear in Oz and get out the implements for making coffee and a calm breakfast, like regular old tourists, or at least legal ones. My ritual: I'd open the rear door and sit at the edge of the seat to inaugurate the visit, to look out over the landscape with my cup steaming.

The first morning in Yosemite, when I still saw Rafael as an unnerving puddle-companion, he settled in beside me and swept a hand toward El Capitan as if to say, this is my house, this is the master bedroom, this is the guest bathroom, this is how you turn on the hot water. He was chatty. In those days, you could never know what to expect, what mood would strike him, what you'd be in for. And what you were in for that morning was this: listening to him talk about El Cap with the familiarity and the weariness of someone who'd made his peace with an inevitable routine. With the tone of someone coming home.

"It's my seventh time. The last time we went up The Heart. Thirty-five pitches and the hardest was a 13b. Fucking ace. See it over there? It looks perfect from here. That pitch leaves you all googly-eyed. The second night we heated a couple cans of red beans, ate, and went to sleep. In the middle of the night we woke up to a sound like a block of stone dropping at top speed. 'Careful, Fabi!'" Rafael looked at me, his eyes wide, imitating the sound of the wind against the stone, reenacting his scramble to get out of the way. If he'd done the same thing that night, it wouldn't have done him much good; when you're sleeping on a vertical wall and something falls from up above, there's nowhere to hide.

"Black and Decker. First I think it's a block, that a piece of the mountain's come off," he recounted with a re-edited expression of panic—a very practiced one, it seemed to me. "That's when I open my eyes," he said, opening them, "and see two bodies falling. 'Fuck, two guys just fell!' I tell Fabi. And then we hear *Pfff*, an explosion. Two rectangles open up and the guys start to fly. Unbelievable."

You turn over in the wrong direction in the middle of the night and you wake with your feet in the air, suspended from the waist, terrified but safe. If you're wearing a harness, that is. If you're not strapped in, you wake in your final flight onto the surface of the planet.

You don't move when you're on the wall. You know where the edge is, and the air. The bed sinks a bit under your weight, which makes the metal tubes on each side of the rectangle a little taller than your body. Those six millimeters reassure you. So, one day, you end up taking off the harness. Then you no longer care whether you're eighty meters up or five hundred. Either way, you'll smash open like a watermelon if you fall. You may as well go for the most dramatic possible splat. Eighty meters. A hundred. Nine hundred. The watermelon shatters no matter what.

That first morning, Rafael, waving a joint in his right hand, was gesturing toward an imaginary line that runs all the way up El Capitan when the water for our second cup of coffee started to boil. He half-turned toward the stove, still imitating the sound of the parachute, now in a lower voice, and pointed a hand—or, better put, the almost-dead joint—toward the granite mass.

"Un...believable."

The next morning, I opened my eyes and found myself alone on the slab. Not a trace of Rafael. I made my way to Oz and found him mid-ritual: coffee, joint, breakfast on the way. That day we ate salami and Emmental cheese sandwiches, thanks to some Germans who'd cut their trip short. He offered me a cup of coffee.

"Today we have to decide which route you're going to climb and who'll go with you."

"I'd like to go solo," said Fabi, who was almost done spreading out and organizing his gear on the ground. "I'd like to do something long."

Rafael raised his eyebrows and said nothing. He pulled the Yosemite climbing guidebook from the depths of the SUV. Nutcracker. Easy and long. Nutcracker. He took out three matches. He broke one of the three, mixed them up, and held them out for each of us to choose one: "The long matches go together and the shortest one figures it out on their own."

I don't remember how high it was. Two hundred meters and change. I only know that it looked very high to me and that I wanted to come down before the halfway point, but we were too far up by then and there was no rope connecting us to the ground. Looking at myself from the outside, I thought about how desperately I wanted to cry. Being the longest climb I'd ever done, I didn't really understand how the rope was supposed to work, what connected to what. I didn't understand why we couldn't rappel. I knew you had to pull the rope, roll it up, hang it from the belay station before continuing upward and reusing it. As you gradually sewed up the route, you'd get farther away from the belay stations, moving right or left. There are no completely straight routes, and so if you tried to rappel, there's no way you would reach the very spot where you'd anchored yourself to go up. But it's one matter to see something right in front of you, understand the logic of what you're looking at, and a very different one to understand it in your cells, in your skin. Only the blind say seeing is believing. It's the other way around: understanding and feeling come first, then digesting, then seeing. That's how it works.

Up on Nutcracker, I thought how reasonable it would be to cry up here, at a such distance from the planet, but my self-pity didn't last long: Rafael was taking photos with his portable camera, which was completely sheathed in duct tape, and I got distracted. "Duct tape! Tape made of ducks," he'd repeat in those days, cracking himself up every single time. He could get pretty one-track. The Basques, the pressure cooker, the duct tape, and so on. As I gained a fuller sense of who he was, and who I was, I'd often tire of his favorite topics, his repetitive jokes, his trains, his commando operations, his taboo bottles. But I never left. Or at least not for long.

In the interests of the financial survival of the family we'd become, we developed the Yosemite photos in a very small format. Little squares like the photobooth kind. I kept all of those portraits next to the letters he wrote me later from Hueco, El Chimborazo, Suesca, Bariloche. That's where I'll store my things from Kathmandu. The DVD. The crystal. Now, whenever I think of the box, I think of the house where the box is. I think of my mother, the closet full of her clothes, which must also be full of dust. I think of my aunts and who will get what. I wonder what I'll find in the drawers of her dressing table. What I'm going to do with her shampoo and conditioner, her medicines. It's not about what you do with things—it's having to hold them in your hands, it's getting your hands sticky with the viscous remnants of shampoo under the bottle cap and knowing that no one else will ever leave those traces behind once you clean it off. It's wondering, as if it mattered, when she'd washed her hair with that shampoo for the last time. It's picking up a shirt, folding it, and wondering how she felt the last time she put it on, standing there with the coat hanger in your hand. I'll toss everything, I tell myself. But not the clothes, I think after a moment. Someone should be able to use them. I wonder about the contents of her dressing table drawers. Everyone has a box full of photos, souvenirs, smaller boxes inside. She always kept everything. She must have kept my postcards, the letters sent by a daughter who was happier the farther away she got.

People compress. Suffocate.

Air. I need air.

But now I think of my mother looking at the landscape, holding the letter or photo in her hand as the illness warped the first of the rest of her cells. How could I keep from wondering exactly when she started to die.

In the first images from Yosemite, I look like a little girl. My hair is disheveled and I seem small. Behind (or below) are the pine trees. Miniscule. I'm always struck by silvery color and the texture of the rock. I can feel the very first brush of the sun's dry rays and the wind on my face, my early astonishment, my numb toes, squeezed into a pair of shoes two sizes too small. From that day onward, the world started to open out through my body and toward the landscape under my feet. A baptism. Those photos contain the beginning of it all: they lead me back to the day when I understood why I am the way I am and what it's for, which puddle is mine, which ecosystem adjusts itself around me.

The landscapes you see from a route that high, you can't see them anywhere else. There's something about the perspective: you look down and find the void beneath your feet and then the gray or the green, almost off-balance, critical, on that incomprehensible scale. Knowing that that scale is your own, remembering that it's where you came from, down below. Understanding that you yourself have been fashioned from such measurements, made of the same materials you can barely discern from where you are, but which you know well; seeing them so inconceivably far away, so inaccessible. Watching the movie and knowing you're outside of it. Breathing and speaking but not entering the world. All of this makes its mark on you. The earth you come from could be Jupiter, for all you know. It doesn't matter. You don't reach it— not it, and not the people who inhabit it. Air.

Up on a wall, there's only the brilliance, the sun heating the surface you ascend, the damp shelf you could slip on. It's just you and this lizard that just darted past you and this cave where you sat down to eat a snack with your feet hanging off the edge, your body swaying like a swing. The planet below. The horizontal line. A meadow. One last phosphorescent hillside, far into the distance. People say that we climbers are always running away from something. That we like danger. They have no fucking idea what they're talking about. It's an arrow-wound, love at first sight. The dazzling of a wild animal in the middle of the night. It hurts; it presses at your chest. Anyone who tells you you're trying to kill yourself doesn't understand a damn thing. Anyone who doesn't get it in time will never get it at all. You're hanging by a thread up there. And you don't want to die. You're afraid for the first ten seconds, afraid to take the first step. Once you're ascending, you don't think about anything else. Just the holds, just about breathing, carrying on. People who want to end it all don't expend so much effort. They throw themselves off a rooftop and that's that. Goodbye. People die in the stupidest ways, in plane crashes, crossing the street. Bathrooms are one of the most dangerous things out there—people fall in the bathtub and die.

Up above, the landscape and your life change in an instant, just like the color of the light. Everything's measured in a single click. It shakes your consciousness, this landscape both remote and heartrending. You look out at it and feel yourself thrum. The landscape sears itself onto your skin.

"Oh, please, for God's sake! You sound like a Hare Krishna," my mom would say.

She never understood that I was talking about photos. 🖼

CHAPTER IX

"You have to feel particles of time. You start to fall in less than a second. You have to look at time with a magnifying glass. To be aware of every thousandth of a second, but without thinking. If you think too much, you fall. It's like dancing. If you think too much, you lose the beat."

It was a discovery on my third trip to Yosemite, an activity for off days or down time. I don't know what it is, but it's not a sport. I owe it to Fabi and the matchsticks. A trip to see how much you can handle. Everyone learns as best they can.

"It's like with everything else, princess. All you have to do is breathe and use your feet. Relax. We adjust the pulleys, the tight-ropes to the biners and rings. Give me that one. Yeah. This one. It's important to protect them like this. Good. We don't want the rope to scrape against the tree. Ready."

He took off his shoes and climbed up.

"Goddammit, let's go!" Rafael shouted up to him from inside Oz, stepping on the gas, making a scene. Rafael had started calling Oz "the quilt." "It won't get us very far, but at least it keeps us warm and dry. It's almost a duvet," he'd say, with slight variations but monothematic as always. "If this thing were more comfortable and less hippie, it would be a duvet. That's what my mom would call it," he'd tell me. "A duvet. But for three hundred bucks? Oz makes it to quilt-status, tops."

"You start here. Feel your soles and your toes. Use your wings. You're less than a meter off the ground, so careful with your ankles. When you're more comfortable, close your eyes. Like this," Fabi showed me, as Rafa kept accelerating and shouting: "The quilt is leaving!"

"Have a smoke when you rest," Fabi told me when we were finished, trying to ignore Rafael and handing me a joint before he lifted his pack to his shoulders. "Enjoy. Soon you'll be able to play wherever you want. Tomorrow it's supposed to be hot again. Tomorrow we'll try at the lake."

He finished off a warm can of beer that was resting on a rock and walked away.

"Wait until the princess is chilling a hundred meters off the surface of the earth, walking through the air from one mountain to the next!" he yelled at Rafael, walking toward him. "She's gonna ditch you!" Laughing, he turned back toward me for the last time and shouted: "You're gonna flip!"

He blew me a kiss.

"Use your *drishti*!" he added.

"Use my what?"

I was hooked for half the day. If you press hard into the rope, you fall. If you don't press hard enough, if you don't apply your weight and intention, you fall. It's fucking hard. You have to flap your arms and find the sweet spot. At first, you lose it as soon as you've got it. You move your arms around in slow motion for a moment or two, you lose your center, and in a fraction of a fraction of a second, you're on the ground. Between your body and where you're going, there's only green grass, air, and a line beneath your feet that you can't look at, but you can feel. You feel the tightrope against the soles of your feet. You're a body in millimetric contraction. Your toes are active without clinging. If you try too hard, you lose; if you clutch, you fall. You return to the present. The present is over; it's already past. Another step. Another. Here and now. With the slightest motion in one of the knots or pulleys, the rope will bounce back on you. But you don't think about that. The dangerous part is fear. You're approaching the other side. If you could only look back. You fix your eyes on a still point that advances little by little, like a cloud in slow motion. A *drishti*.

"You have to look for beauty from inside your veins, from your muscles and your skin toward the rock, toward the air, toward the street," said Fabi on the night of my first tightrope crossing as Rafa played music and rolled a joint. We were all celebrating. Everyone was celebrating something different. I was happy.

People get up every morning, take a shower, get dressed, go to school or to work, spend hours socializing, fall in love, get married, have families, home sweet home. Over time, they stay in love or they don't, they stay put or they don't, their loved ones die or they don't. But with their families they try to recreate or avoid, at all costs, whatever kind of order they've learned. They learn to live that way. Which never worked for me. If you get in a jam on the rock with a wedding ring, you lose a finger. If your hands swell after a long day of climbing, the ring gets stuck, your blood stops circulating, it hurts for hours. You have to string it on a chain around your neck or leave it at home. People say you're born alone and you die alone, but that's not true. You're born in the company of others and it happens in a split second. Someone's erased. Without anesthesia. People tell you you're born alone and you die alone, but it's not true.

"Incredible," he said, pulling me by the harness from the edge of the wall, toward him, when I finished my first tightrope walk.

Fabi at one side of the precipice. Rafael at the other end of the rope. Me, about to finish the cross. Reaching the other side. "Incredible," he said. "Un...believable. A bird. With these little wings," he added, lifting my arms at my sides.

"A cat," I answered. "It's more feline than anything else. Right, Fabi?" I yelled toward the other end of the void. "It's all about the little pillows in the feet. You have to try it," I started to say, just as he leaned forward and kissed me, abruptly, interrupting me, silencing me by force.

"And the ass!" Fabi hollered, laughing. "If you don't squeeze in your ass, you fall!"

"I don't like cats," said Rafael in a low voice, after he'd let me go and put a few steps between us. No one answered him. Fabi looked at us from a distance. We laughed. Fabi and I.

Rafa kept walking away. 卐

Chapter X

Rafael shared an apartment in Berkeley with Fabi and a Chilean guy I barely spoke to at first. Rafael and Fabi called him the Nerd, but not to make fun of him; it was to make fun of me. I was still in college. The Chilean would leave the apartment very early every morning and shut himself up in his room when he came home at the end of the day. He was afraid of us. Weeks passed and I still didn't really know him at all. Until the night I found him making instant ramen in the kitchen. He was a physicist. He'd left behind a girlfriend in Santiago and his glasses shielded a pair of intensely green eyes, the color of the water at Los Roques.

As for us, we'd rarely wake up before ten in the morning, and it was around midday, after breakfast, by the time we'd go off to climb, with a thermos of sweet black coffee in tow. Sometimes, though, we'd leave before dawn, bringing only the same thermos of coffee and a stash of fruit and candy.

Otherwise, as they set routes and spotted clients at the gym, or carried wood panels and mixed cement, I'd clean the houses of climber friends or their other friends. Normal people's houses, if you could use the word "normal" to describe the hacker I once worked for before I abruptly stopped showing up. I got to choose. Eight dollars an hour didn't fund a whole trip, but they pooled into what I already had, and into what they already had, and our savings slowly grew. When I started teaching Spanish classes, everything got even easier. Twelve, fifteen bucks an hour. Totally different. I felt sorry for Rafa and Fabi—they'd come home covered in dust, their hair all gray, their faces streaked with plaster or soot. With that unmistakable funk, their worker-smell of labor and sweat. Pale faces, no earth or sun for their bodies. No pleasure.

"Today we had to sand the whole fucking house."

After a shower, they'd devote themselves to eating with a violent hunger and smoking joint after joint until they were comatose. We'd often watch a chaotic succession of climbing or BASE jumping videos until our eyes glazed over with weed and repetition, slides depicting places that turned into plans, plans that were both more accessible than ever (we had money) and still unreachably far away (we had jobs).

"Bird, I'll go crazy if I don't get out of here."

He'd finish a gig and disappear. The Russian mafioso would leave messages for him. "The house that needs sanding in Sacramento is now or never. These people don't wait," the Russian would say in a voicemail I could only hear if I found the cell phone with the smashed, illegible screen under a sofa cushion, between the seats in Oz, or jumbled in with the climbing gear. The light flickering. By the time I listened to the message, we were already on the highway, reaching Yosemite. Why would I tell Rafael that the Russian guy had called him when we'd already been at Red Rocks for ten days? After the trip, we'd find different jobs. Another house to move. Another house to clean or sand. Another opportunistic mobster. New students or the same ones. Sometimes they'd wait for me. If you asked Rafael, with or without some money in his pocket, he'd tell you we were millionaires.

"We're rich in red blood cells, Bird."

I went back to Caracas twice. The first was to resume my biology studies. And the second was to finish my thesis and be with my mom. At the end. Rafa and Fabi would return when they were sick, when they got into a bad accident, and very rarely just to visit their parents.

Living without medical insurance when you spend all your time hanging from a rope demands strength and clarity, real control, careful attention. You have to take care of yourself. There's something showy about plunging down onto the planet.

"They'd better never rescue you in a helicopter. No matter what. I've seen it. No one asks you a damn thing here. They're melodramatic. They love it when the ambulance comes. They force you to get in, they make you believe it's free, and then it's a huge fucking mess. They start sending you the bills. The assholes won't leave you alone. Bam, two thousand bucks. You have to watch out."

Once a Polish guy fractured his shoulder blade on the Half Dome and there was no way to get him off the wall. He wouldn't get into the helicopter. He and his wife refused to let go and there was nothing to be done. If you don't want to be rescued, they can't rescue you.

"That's how it is, Bird. Don't you forget it. No one can make anyone come down off a wall. No one can force you to get saved."

Sometimes I'd wake up in the morning to an empty house. I'd spend hours alone, thinking they were at the construction site or the gym—until night fell or several days had passed. Sometimes Fabi and I were the ones to drive off and get lost in Oz. On the day of Sex Porpoises, we were lost for a whole day. We stopped at a supermarket on the way back.

In the parking lot, Fabi rubbed his hands together and held them to his mouth, exhaling to heat them up.

"You have to take advantage of evenings like this," he said. "It'll be cold soon, seriously cold. There'll be ice. Stay put, don't bother parking," he added. "I'll be right back." A few minutes later, I saw him cutting across the parking lot, empty-handed. Not a single bag. He looked both ways. He got into the car, asked me to start the engine without answering the obligatory question, and lifted his sweater once we were on the highway. Twenty-seven chocolate bars tumbled down between the seats and the emergency brake, onto the rug in the back, onto our feet. Cadbury. Snickers. Milky Way. Toblerone. It was wild.

"I'll have the white one, please."

"Shit, Fabi!"

He wasn't stealing chocolate, he explained to me later, not looking at me, his mouth full, wide eyes fixed on the road. He said something about acts of anarchy. You have to rebel against the system. No one cares about us here. We're invisible.

He said this and other things about construction work and immigrant life. His jaws grinding hard, muscles expanding sideward, like gills.

"Do you understand what six dollars an hour means? Okay, you're training, you're training with every bag of cement you carry on your back, you get stronger. And six dollars is better than no dollars, let's be clear about that. But goddammit, Julia! Six fucking dollars?" He wadded up the Toblerone wrapper and tossed it onto the back seat. I could hear his saliva and his bones with every bite.

His rage lasted as long as it took him to eat the last piece. "But today is today. We have to celebrate today's climb," he said in a different tone, smiling, patting me twice on the thigh. "Sex Porpoises, huh? You're a tough one, you know. You're quite the Little Miss Mountain Goat, aren't you?" and he laughed.

"And where did all this come from?" Rafael asked when he arrived and found us sitting on the floor, surrounded by chocolate wrappers and wrinkled papers of all brands and colors, our gear spread out on the blanket.

"It's all mine, so watch it," I replied with a smile that Rafael didn't return. "I won it. My prize. Didn't I? Sex Porpoises on-sight."

Not answering, Rafael sat down on the couch to watch a football game on TV.

"From the bottom to the top without falling?" he said minutes later, eyes steady on the screen.

"From the bottom to the top without falling."

Rafa stood and paced around the living room like a caged animal.

"Shit. Something smells like shit here," he said finally, and he took a deep sniff before he walked out the apartment door without saying where he was going. He returned almost an hour later, blazed, with a six-pack that was missing three beers; he took it into the room. The Chilean guy showed up soon after and sat down with Fabi and me. He didn't stay long; he said something about Emiliana, that he had to call her, and he left, nervous as he always was when there were other people around.

"Aw...I feel bad. Julia's got a crush on the Nerd," said Rafael as he reentered the room, just when the Chilean had disappeared into his.

"He's calling his girlfriend," I answered. "And what's with you? Were you just standing in the doorway and waiting for him to leave?"

"At least someone has one, right? A girlfriend, I mean. Or boyfriend. No one else has one here. That's for sure." He let his comment take effect and swallowed it with another gulp of beer, stood at the window, smoked a Marlboro he'd gotten who knows where. And before he retreated back into his cave, he answered Fabi, who was asking him about the climbing plans for the week:

"Ask Julia. Take Julia," he said, and banged the table with his lighter. He hit it hard. I thought it would break. "Or maybe I should say, I don't know why the fuck you're asking me. I'm sure you guys already have it all planned out. Admit it. Come on. Let me know," he said before the final door-slam of the day. And from inside his room: "If you fucking feel like it, I mean."

Grizzly bears seem like one thing, but they're totally different. They seem like noble savages, but they're blunt, brutal animals. If they hug you, they crush you.

I started to feel like I had to be on my guard. He seemed irritable, barely spoke to me. Around the same time, they started working with the Russian guy in Sacramento again, so everything froze. They'd show up in the evening like zombies, shower, smoke a couple joints, drink three beers, go to sleep. I let go, forgot my wariness. Which was stupid. Sometimes fear is useful. As long as it doesn't paralyze you; so long as your antenna still works. Whatever, it's all bullshit, I thought then. What you can't see doesn't exist. Nothing's wrong.

The Chilean wasn't bad-looking at all. He had a girlfriend, so he didn't want anything serious, but he was lonelier than the moon. And he was very close by. Ten steps from my bed. You get tired of the threats and stop believing them. What could happen? I wondered. Nothing, I answered. When you see yourself bounce back like a rubber band once, you think you're capable of reacting on time. You think you can save yourself no matter what. When you see that you haven't died, you think you'll never die. When it's my turn, it's because it was my turn. Like my mom. A regular middle-aged woman. Instead of it happening to me or one of the weirdos I call friends, she's the one who went and died—the one who'd get into her car every morning to work all day, come home in the afternoon or at night to water the plants on the balcony, take care of her daughter when her daughter let herself be taken care of, watch a soap opera, and go to bed.

I discovered how much I liked to rankle him, push him until exploded, see how far he'd go. It never occurred to me that there aren't just deaths and endings; there are also wounds, injuries, fractures, fissures. Abuses. Marks. When it's time, it's time, I'd tell myself. They switch off the light on you and that's that. Bam. It's over. That's what was floating around in the atmosphere, around my head, like a cloud.

How naïve.

One Friday afternoon, Rafael came back to the apartment earlier than usual and found us, as he put it, being sketchy. It wasn't so much what he said as how close he got to me when he said it. It seemed ridiculous at the time, but I thought he was about to bite me on the cheek. I shrank back.

"Are you guys saving water or something? Is Berkeley suddenly Caracas? Is there a water shortage?" he demanded, and he touched my wet hair, looking at the Chilean guy's from a distance. That Sunday, he went out for groceries and sniffed me when he came back. He seized me by the hair and pushed me backward, pulling at my neck before he licked it all the way up to my chin and bit me there, on my lower jaw. Like a bear, a hunting dog.

"Have you ever taken a good look at my hands?" he asked me that night as he peeled an orange. "They say it's easy. That you press into the neck, like this," he said, extracting a wedge, "and that's it. It's hard at first, but then no one's kicking anymore and all that's left is one final push against the floor. It's easy," he concluded. He chewed half an orange slice intently. "That's what they say."

Jaws are incredible. Crushing machines. 牙

Chapter XI

We went to Red Rocks during the time they were finishing the Sacramento gig to celebrate my birthday. Rafael said he had a surprise for me. We arrived around midnight, set up the tent with our headlamps on, and crashed right away. On the first morning, a bowl of oatmeal and a four-hour walk to Levitation 29. My birthday present. A vertical 11c of slabs like fish scales the color of sand and dark coffee. Radiant, perfect. It's clear that a landscape is like a person: it changes you, alters your perspective. You leave a place and you're not the same. You can't just leave it behind; the landscape comes with you. A place with light like the light at Levitation 29 doesn't just vanish from your memory. When I reached the wall, I felt like a dust particle, my heart swelling up before the mountain and its orange light, its lead-colored veins. I walked up to a big boulder, maybe twice my height. I scaled it in two or three steps and stayed there. I couldn't move.

"I feel like I'll die if I go up there," I said, glancing at Rafael and feeling a flash of fear that was more like an omen of what was already brewing, or what was already written but hadn't yet occurred.

"Bird. Go up. It'll pass."

I can't explain it. It had never happened to me before and hasn't ever happened again. I felt weak: my chest heaving, on the verge of tears, my throat stiffened into a block. I hid behind my hands, leaning my forehead against my bent knees.

Rafael looked at me from the base of the route. He glanced back and forth between the mountain and his own feet, hands on his hips, not saying a word. At a certain time of day, according to Rafael, depending on the direction of the sunlight, you can see an eagle made of shadows on the rock's southern face. And it's supposed to be beautiful.

We ended up going back. It took us seven and a half hours to retrace the path that had taken us four on the way there. He barely looked at me. I thought he must be annoyed about the pointless hike. Maybe he felt rejected. He didn't speak.

"The wall looked gorgeous. I don't know why, but I don't feel well. I don't think I've eaten enough. It's like I feel weak."

Nothing. He just walked, wordless.

"I'm sorry, Rafael," I told him later. I apologized for not properly receiving my gift.

It all fit together in the end. Every piece played its part. Clockwork. Say Rafael plus Julia and the Chilean guy. Say Julia in Peru, or any male name next to mine on a trip without Rafael, and all other words are superfluous. The story tells itself. There's no phone at Red Rocks. In theory, we didn't ask questions. When we'd travel without calling each other, there were no questions. There's no cell reception at Red Rocks. There's no park ranger at Red Rocks, no trees, not even the smallest pool of water. He could easily go off somewhere and come back with a girl, or not come back at all. Red Rocks is a red maze. I used to tell myself that what you don't name doesn't exist. I'd tell myself: don't say fear and you won't be afraid. But it doesn't matter. There are places where shouting is a futile gesture.

An owl lost in the darkness.

He made a carbonara that we ate out of the pot in silence. He lay down beside me in the tent, stroking my face, my hair.

"It's easy for me. You know that, right?" He spoke tenderly. "I could kill you right here and no one would know. I could dig into your throat, right here, and that would be that. It would be your fault. For being a slut. I could stick you into one of these cracks, and you tell me, who would come looking? The Chilean guy?"

I tried to sit up.

His thumbs hard against my neck, his hands, the same hands he used in bed with me and at the construction site and on the crystal ledges on the wall and to roll a joint. The same hands as his hands on the safety, adjusting the harness, setting up my bed on the rock wall. The rough hands that kept me safe (you won't fall as long as I'm here, Bird). A sharp pain in the Adam's apple. And then the apple disappears. A whimper.

"But not so fast. Right?" He released my neck. "Because I want some of this first. Some of the sweetness you give that fucking Nerd. Are you going to give it to me?" He lowered his hand, jammed it under my pants' elastic waist, put his fingers inside me. Sand.

My jaws are strong, too. You can be squeezing them together and not even notice. On a route. In a moment of rage, of helplessness. I used them that night. I gained momentum and bit him on the neck. I pushed him, although I doubted there was any need for that. I wasn't sure whether my own life depended on me, whether it was all really happening. I could let myself be overtaken and tomorrow would be another day, I thought, as I bit him and shoved him toward the other side of the tent. Doubting. Feeling melodramatic, outside of myself. At least he didn't have his hands between my legs anymore. Maybe it's better if I let him, I remember thinking. If I let him, I'm sure he won't do anything, I thought, after he swung himself back onto me again. The hairs on my back stiff as an urchin, my teeth like metal shards. I opened my eyes as wide as I could.

"What the fuck is wrong with you? Are you crazy?" I tried to swing out my arms like a pair of antlers, arched my fingers into claws, and went straight for his eyes. "Fuck, Rafael! Leave me alone!"

If someone closes his eyes very tightly, you can't reach them. You can't sink into them. It's the sort of thing you never think about.

I tried to put space between us. I shoved at him with my flexed legs and he changed tacks, grabbing under my pants again. He managed to pull them down. I was still trapped under his weight. There's nothing worse than thinking you're stronger than you really are.

I wanted to bite him on the ear, and I thought of the early rumors about him, the stories whispered along the curves of the traverse, the warnings I got from Lupe and Tomás. I thought of that unknown woman. I saw myself in the photo of that nameless girlfriend. I thought of how difficult it was to defend yourself and I decided it was right. Biting him was the best I'd be able to do. In an instant, Rafael froze, stunned by the sight of the tarp darkened by our silhouettes. Thank you. I thanked the woman, the red rocks of that place. My star. Calm is coming.

But Rafael was gathering his strength. He needed a moment to breathe before putting an end to it all.

"What do you want me to tell you? Rafael's complicated," Fabi would say.

"If you were my sister, I'd forbid you," Tomás would say. "Even though he's like my brother."

"The Argentine girl says he's an asshole," Lupe said once.

I wanted to cry, but I couldn't.

"Bird, you and I are exactly the same."

I remembered his words and it was like a volcano. I rammed at him with my feet, with my hands. I heaved myself onto him. War cry. I smashed the lantern against his head. When you do something like that, you have to be careful, because it's another of those things you never think about: you hurt yourself when you're trying to hurt someone else. I cut him across the forehead, but I also cut my hand. He punched me.

There are places where shouting is a futile gesture. There are no park rangers at Red Rocks. There's no phone. The Wizard of Oz was far away. In theory, when you don't ask questions, they don't ask you, either.

There, in that place, remained my bruised trachea; a leaky eye, an eye that kept weeping for several days; a certain fear of the dark. I was repulsed by my own thighs; they felt flabby for a long time. Silence remained the only language. Intermittent or sporadic waves of nausea.

"All of this is your fault," he said calmly, pointing at me, still threatening me with his index finger after he'd pulled up his pants with rage and before he stepped out into the darkness. "Now you're going to say I'm an asshole. But you've been deep in this shit for weeks. You asked for it."

I stayed inside the tent, and I left it open so I could keep watch. I stared out the door for hours, fearing a third and final round. Then I did leave the tent—to vomit. The highway was at least two hours from there. It must have been around five in the morning when I emerged with the rising sun. He was some ten meters away, crouching on the ground, smoking, gazing at the fiery snail that is Red Rocks at that time of day. Any reflection hurt my eye, so even if I had no way of seeing myself, I imagined I looked awful.

"Don't go, Julia," he said, turning around, still on his knees, looking up at me from the dirt. I shone the lantern right into his face. One eye was swollen. He fixed me with the other. "Don't go, little Bird." He stretched out as if to drag himself on the ground, grabbed my ankles before I could try to run. It was a pointless gesture. I lacked the strength even to walk, and I didn't want to leave. If I had my way, I'd have curled up on my side, staring into the void, the red turtles along the yellow flatland, the bluest sky I'd ever seen.

I'd have lain completely motionless, observing the contrast between the blue and the orange, the accidental cacti. I would have
stayed still as a plant.

I didn't feel like talking or crying. It was my fault, I told myself.
Nice going, I told myself. You wanted to hurt him and now you're
the one who's all fucked up. There you go. To some extent, I didn't
care about any of it; it all felt like someone else's story. My head
ached. I felt nauseated again, but also hungry, and when I thought
of eating I stood up to vomit again. My shoulders weighed heavily
on me. My abductors throbbed, my thighs, my vulva. I must have
been in pretty bad shape, because it hurt even to turn toward the
light. My hips were sore, too.

"I couldn't help it," he said when I sat down beside him, and
he reached out to touch my eye, my hair. I suddenly thought
that everything had begun exactly like this: with a caress just
like this one, mere hours before. There we were. The worst was
over.

I left my things on the ground as if they were a hostage secur-
ing my presence there. We both knew that if I'd wanted to go, I
would have, leaving everything behind. Objects don't matter when
everything hurts. I walked away. When I turned around to look,
I saw him disassembling the tent and piling everything up beside
my pack. He made a breakfast I struggled to swallow. The sand
had migrated to my mouth, my jaws didn't respond, my injured
hand pulsed. I felt fat and repulsed by everything, and my throat
was inflamed. All the better. So you won't eat, I said to myself. My
eye shut. After the first few mouthfuls, I threw up again.

"Another try?" he asked, his eyes fixed on the vertical wall.

We started to walk. When we were close to the way out of the
park, I slowed down. He followed.

"Give me the keys," I said. Gaze on the ground. Heavy thighs and
ankles. Shoulders abandoned to the earth.

He came to a halt.

"Yeah. I think we should rest. We can go if you want."

"The papers? Do you have them? And the keys. Give me the keys." The door was close. Twenty meters. Thirty tops. Park rangers. Phone booth. The best way to hide your fear is to move. You have to keep your hands moving so no one can see them shake.

"You're not going to see the Chilean guy anymore," he said, handing me the keys. "We'll get out of that house. Everything's going to get better, we'll go somewhere else, far away from Fabián and the fucking Chilean. Get going. Go on home and do what you need to do. It's all good, Bird. Have you noticed the way Fabi looks at you? You seem tired, Bird. Look. It's easy. We'll find a new place." He grabbed me by the arm and pulled me toward him hard enough for me to whimper. My skin shrank back again and my back stiffened into a hook. I squeezed my eyes shut and the pain sharpened.

"I'll see you there," he added, releasing me. "You're going straight back." He put his sunglasses onto my face. "Don't take them off. You know what to do," he insisted. His eyes were very wide. He held the key out to me.

"Mm-hm."

"I'll see you at the house. Go straight home, Bird. Don't you get lost on the way there."

I walked faster, craning my neck to look behind me. The tips of my shoes skittered on the sand. And I kept glancing back. The habit's never left me. I always tell myself that it's in case I've left any gear behind, if there's any trash to pick up, if I've left everything exactly as it was when I got there. I kept finding him in exactly the same spot, smaller and smaller. With a motionless hand raised in the air in the end. A daguerreotype. I left the keys to Oz on top of the same tire as always.

Sugar in the radiator. People say it works like a charm. That's what Rafael swore later. That when he tried to start up Oz, it wouldn't start up, and everything smelled like caramel. Like molasses taffy, he said. "Someone put sugar in the radiator. Is there anyone alive who understands you, Bird? You're a tricky one. No Oz for you now."

I made my way back to the apartment by bus. Dazed. I bolted inside. I stuffed my things into my backpack as best I could. I opened the drawer of documents, pulled out mine, and my ticket, and tore out the stamped pages in Rafael's passport. Without thinking. I took a shower and scrubbed my thighs, my crotch, slid a soapy finger inside myself. I scoured my fingers and toes. I shaved, sitting on the floor. Before I got out, I wiped the loofa across my hips and inner thighs again. When I was out of the bathroom, I found a pair of scissors, returned to the parachute pack, and sank the blades into the cloth. I didn't see how far, but I didn't think it was far enough—better go all the way—so I pulled the cloth outward as best I could, ripping it farther, and yes, there, I thought, that looks about right. I turned the wings over to hide the hole. I had no time to regret what I'd done or even to think. When I had everything ready, I heard the door creak. You feel like a cat: the hairs on your back stand up and your spine contorts. I tossed my bag under the bed. When I realized I was still holding the scissors, I threw them in the same direction. I heard their voices, both of them. The sound of the gear dropping to the ground, the fridge door opening, the continuation of a conversation I couldn't make out. I had to dash out to the bathroom. When Rafa came in, he found me wrapped in a towel and leaning over the toilet bowl. He reached for me, gripped me by the forehead. I arched like a greyhound and vomited saliva.

"Leave me alone a second," I said, but he didn't. He pulled me up from the floor, wiped off my face, dried it. He passed the towel across my eye, my neck. He had a piece of gauze on his forehead.

"I'll be outside."

I put on my sunglasses and a striped scarf he'd given me as a gift. There were little daisies by the sofa and chocolate cookies on the table. They were both standing there, looking toward the bedroom door.

"Aha! Finally!" Fabi said.

"Close your eyes."

"Come on! Close your eyes!"

I ripped your passport, I thought. If you jump with those wings, you're done.

"Close your *eyes*," he insisted.

I ripped your passport. If you jump with those wings, you're done. Swift movements after the sound of cloth. Laughter.

"Ready! Okay. You can open them."

Fabián was looking at me as if everything were completely normal. Playing dumb. As if he knew nothing. And that, goddammit, was impossible. He'd picked up Rafael at the bus station; he'd probably taken him to the hospital. There's no way he hadn't asked about his injury, or about me. Where's the princess? he must have asked him. What the hell did you do to get *that*? There's no way it's from climbing, he had to have told Rafael. It was obvious. And now I was wearing a scarf and sunglasses in the middle of the living room. But no. Nothing. Close your eyes, he told me. Motherfucker.

"There's no way you're staying here all by yourself—come with us, sweetie," he added, as if it were a normal thing to address me so paternalistically in this house, to fret over me, to worry about leaving me on my own. "Come on," he insisted, and he held up a package just like Rafael's, though his was green. My body felt very heavy but I didn't want to stay; I was afraid of being alone. Or of refusing to go with them, which isn't the same thing.

Rafael had a new set of wings.

He drove. I fell asleep in the back, curled up, after we stopped for two six-packs. We headed toward the outskirts of the city. Crossing two bridges, we ended up parked in a silent housing development. Or maybe it was the time of night when every suburb goes silent. Rafa and Fabi dug around for their packages. We cut across the dark, narrow street, made our way over three barbed-wire fences. We waked through several black hills. There were only shadows: ours, and the shadow cast by an electrical antenna we moved toward, trying to limit our noise to the swish of our packs and our jackets, the tread of our feet on the grass. We ascended the flimsy aluminum stairs. We didn't speak.

"Careful or you'll fall."

I nodded and let out a hollow laugh. My legs were trembling. When we were nearing the top, Fabián came to halt. He bowed and stayed there, readying his parachute from the second-to-last step. At the peak, Rafael opened his backpack, singing "Rompe Saragüey," shimmying to the beat. He spread out the cloth on the ground as he danced, and he looked more like a sorcerer casting a spell than an extreme athlete on the verge of springing into action. I wondered how he could possibly feel like dancing. How many times had he hit people and then sashayed around the world like this. I felt like I was part of a different map: I was with the others there. With the ones who had feared him and potentially tried to defend themselves. A new category. New sub-genus. New puddle. He cracked open one more beer and emptied it in five or six swigs. He left the can in the tower.

"Here I go!" I heard below me.

Rafael gripped me by the waist and I hung outward, entrusting my weight to his forearm, extending my torso into the dark void. The green Fox floating and landing a little farther ahead.

"Beau. Ti. Ful."

A few seconds later, he was also on the edge.

"Good. Here I go."

He started to count, uttered something I couldn't understand, stretched out his body, extended his arms, and stepped out into the abyss. I barely saw it happen. Everything's very fast in the air. The sound of the cloth whooshing again. I drew a little closer, but lying down on the platform this time. I thought of the broken wings in the dark apartment, wondered when it would be their turn. I should tell him, I thought. I descended the rickety stairs. I didn't like being alone there. They were packing up down below.

"Come on, fast, let's go."

We got into the SUV in commando mode.

"Classy shit, Fabi. Beers and tacos at the Mexican place?"

The next morning, the bed was empty. The old Foxes and the new ones were still there. So were the Five Tens and the harnesses. They couldn't have gone far. I had coffee for breakfast, the remnants of a cigarette abandoned in the kitchen astray. There was a plastic bag from the pharmacy, a foundation compact. I thought the hue of the makeup would be too pale for my skin, but it turned out to be just right. I started to cut my fingernails at the bathroom mirror and then I stopped; I thought I might need them later. I ate a piece of chocolate off a little plate beside the ashtray. I read an article in the New Age magazine we'd use to unwind and thought about the three layers of the brain and which ones were most active in mine. The reptilian one, definitely. I had to get out of there. No goodbyes. Today was the day. To split, I thought, before I bolted to the bathroom and threw up. I curled up in bed again and fell asleep, thinking of how urgent it was: time to go. Time to feel better. I woke to the sound of the zippers, the plastic bags, the gear.

"I ran into the Japanese guys," he said, barely taking the time to look at me when I peered in through the doorway. A group of Japanese climbers I didn't know and still don't. I could hardly open my eye.

"They're all ready to go and they have an extra spot. Have you seen my Boreals? And they need someone who speaks Spanish and knows their way around the jungle." He approached me, took hold of my jaw, inspected my eye. He said nothing. "In the flesh! The man himself! That's me!" he said, raising his voice so sharply that I flinched. "What's the matter with you, Bird? It's like you're scared of me or something. *Ya yo sé que te gustó / quieres bailarlo otra vez / báilalo en la punta'el pie / y verás qué bueno es.* Shit, I know I left them around here somewhere. Think the Chilean could've walked off with them? You know, I think that Chilean's probably training behind our backs," he laughed.

Fabián watched him from a distance as he twirled a lighter in circles on the table like a game of spin-the-bottle. As if there were something to be said. He didn't say it. Hours later, I learned that he'd asked Rafael when he was leaving and who were they, any-way—where had the Japanese guys come from all of the sudden. Why hadn't he requested a spot for Fabi, too. For him, he said. A couple hours before, I'd decided to walk out the door and disap-pear, and now I'd lost my chance. I thought of Caracas and the uni-versity and my mom as I waited for Rafael to enter the room where I'd sequestered myself, to sit down beside me, to apologize. If he comes in, I'll tell him about the wings. "Goddammit! The Boreals! You sure you haven't seen them?" he yelled from the living room. "Fuck, my boots!"

I heard him shut the door without saying goodbye. People can leave. Whatever. But you have to say goodbye, dammit. Before Fa-bián and I left for Yosemite, I pulled the fucking boots out from under my pillow and threw them into the trash.

"You told him about the Chilean guy."

"Leave me out of this, Julia. You're a ballsy one, you know that? The Chilean—you've got to be kidding me. The Chilean, who's a fucking nerd on top of everything else."

After ten days in Yosemite, tightrope-walking and climbing gentle routes without ever mentioning Rafael's name or the ar-gument on the highway, we parted ways with the knowledge that we wouldn't see each other again for a long time. He had a girl-friend in Caracas, who knows how, who only spoke ten words of English and zero of Spanish. A Swedish girl, as it turned out. That's what I heard them say on a traverse: "It's amazing! A girl who climbs and doesn't talk. She's either Swedish or she's playing dumb."

I called my mother once I was back from Yosemite.

"Everything's fine here, sweetheart. And what about you? How are you? When are you coming home?" She insisted that her hoarseness was due to a virus. "Everything's a virus these days."

When you know, you know.

"I just bought my ticket yesterday," I improvised. "I really have to finish my thesis." I'd thought about it long and hard and she was right, I said. I had to close one chapter before starting the next.

I could tell she was puzzled and pleased to hear her own words in my voice. Before I left the apartment, I flipped over the parachute backpack and ripped harder at the hole so that it would be even more obvious. So it wouldn't go unseen. ◫

Chapter XII

"It's always important to dress to the nines," she'd say, as she passed a hand across her chest, tugged briskly at her pants, inspected her freshly painted nails. She'd speak with pride, recurring to our feminine family tree: "Because we've always been very chic." "Are you really going out like that?" seemed to be her favorite parting comment. "It's not that hard, missy. It just takes two minutes," she'd say, arming herself with a hair dryer when she saw me walk out with wet hair. "See? Look how pretty you are. You turned out just like your grandmother María Angélica—flat as a board. But it's better that way. You look like a dancer. It's a European look."

She wasn't easy.

"You don't have any fun, Mom. Look at how nice the light is this morning. Take Saturday off! Don't do anything. Get out of your bad mood! Breathe! Want to come to La Guairita?" it once occurred to me to ask her.

"Oh, great! That's just what I need! An invitation to lounge around in the woods, with mosquitos and snakes, watching you perched in a tree like yet other wild animal."

"What tree, Mom? What are you talking about?"

She spent her life solving other people's problems: my cousins, her siblings. Mine, too, she thought. She tried to take care of me. She spent her life working because she had no choice, but if she had, she would have spent it working just the same.

"If there's one thing no one can take away from me, it's that I raised you myself, I supported you myself. And I don't owe that, we don't owe that, to anyone. Carlos is out there with his family. And we're here, you and me. And we lacked for nothing, did we?

"No."

When I'd made up my mind to study biology, after a failed semester in social communications and almost switching to geology, she told me I should think it over. That gorillas and ants don't put food on the table; that they're all about *looking* for food. That researchers live lonely lives, that they never get out of the lab, out of the swamp. And that no interesting man (which meant *of status*) would have anything to do with a girl who was streaked with dirt and reeking of sweat. That I'd only keep landing unpresentable hippies. And that love never lasts if you're hungry.

"Between the climbing and biology, you're going to get lost in the jungle one of these days. You know that? By the time I was your age..."

"I know. By the time I was your age, you already had me. But things are different now! Relax, Mom. Go out with your girlfriends," I'd tell her. "If you don't want to come with me, go out with them!"

At a certain point, I was done. I'd sling my pack onto my shoulder, give her a kiss on the forehead, on the cheek, and I'd be off.

"We'll just see what you do with those little animals of yours when you have children. When your husband leaves you for another woman and you have to support yourself. I'd like to see you do that. Feed your kids, maintain a household. Look at me! Learn from what's right in front of you! All alone! You're going to end up all alone with your monkeys and your ants one day, and then you'll see!" The sermon didn't stop until I was out the door and stayed away for a few hours.

And as far as Rafael was concerned, she was merciless. "Not even this much," she'd say, pressing her thumb and index finger together. "He doesn't love you even this much. One thing's for sure; you're going to end up killing each other," she'd declare. "Go find yourself a boyfriend who takes you out for sushi, for a walk, who takes you somewhere nice. Not this! Just look at you. You neglect yourself, honey, when you hang out with people like him. Look at those hands, look at your nails."

What's funny is that people swore we were exactly alike.

I run to the subway station, dart down the stairs. I swipe my card but the machine rejects it, sounding its raspy buzzer. I swipe it again and again. I lose my patience and the card bends in half. I fume. I hear the subway doors opening. I can't get through. The error noise keeps blaring. I vault the turnstile and run. I zigzag around the passengers; they move slowly, crossing each other's paths. I leap up the stairs two at a time. The passengers exist in another plane, another film being shot in slow motion. When I get there, the doors have just snapped shut. I peer in through the window. I search the car with my eyes and find my sick mother. I know she's sick, because she's wearing pajamas, mis-buttoned, and has an IV drip in her hand. She looks pretty good, all things considered. She has hair. I press my hands against the glass and look at her. She lifts her palm to me and offers me a half-smile, saying goodbye. The train starts moving.

Weeks after I came to the city, Lupe and Caboose invited me to Mérida. We went without much of a plan. We drove all night and arrived early. Straight to the market. *Pisca* soup, a few meat and chicken *pastelitos*. *Cocadas* and *dulce de leche*. Smoked cheese. Andean *arepas*. Raw cane sugar and granola. We continued on to

5,007. Pico Bolívar was once five thousand seven meters high. The peak has been gradually melting: it's now four thousand nine hundred ninety-eight meters, and people argue about it. Some say it's ninety-eight, others ninety-five. But the mountaineering store where you buy the rest of your gear, where you meet up with your friends and plan the route you're about to climb, is still called 5,007.

I found out about Rafa without asking. From Tomás, who heard it from Fabi. That he jumped off El Capitan again and fractured an ankle. That he got a new job. That his photos were published in *Rock and Ice*, that you should go buy this month's *Climbing* or next month's; that he'll appear in its pages any minute now, ascending Half Dome.

"We'll take a day to get used to the altitude, find some boots and pants for Lupe, and buy everything else we need. Zero stress. We'll go up on Wednesday," Caboose had proposed that time in Mérida, "and we'll be back in six days."

I made arrangements with my aunts and left. We stayed with Raúl. We partied at La Cucaracha on the first night. On the second, some people came over and we stayed up till dawn. The usual: Leo with his slides from the Cordillera, another guy with some from the Chimborazo. I brought some photos from Red Rocks, the ones from Mickey's Beach, and a few others from La Guairita with Lupe. For the second day in a row, we woke up—absurdly late—concluding that there was no way we could go up today with a hangover this bad, but tomorrow for sure. And every day we'd open up our backpacks to take something else out. Our gear, which got in the way as we rummaged, ended up strewn around the room in accordance with how much it obstructed us from getting to whatever we were looking for. As if by inertia, it shifted toward the walls and corners. Sluggish in the postponement of everything, and indifferent to any plan that didn't involve parties and friends, we ate the food that emerged. In the order it emerged in. If the first thing was a bag of oatmeal from the market, dried peaches, parmesan cheese, and pasta, then we knew what awaited us that day. Cans of tuna. *Arepas*. Chocolate. Whatever we found was welcome. We spent several nights cooking special dinners at Leo's house. Berry wine, fettuccine Alfredo, lentils and rice, *arepas* with tuna. We'd listen to music, smoke, stay up all night again. The next day, we'd make a late breakfast and tell ourselves the very same thing. Can't do it today. Tomorrow for sure.

The few city clothes we'd brought ended up scattered all over the house. I eventually had to wear a shirt of Lupe's; Raúl, a pair of my socks that kept drooping downward and curled around the arches of his feet. Because our host lived hand to mouth, sprawled out on a sleeping mat and sheltered only by a sleeping bag. Whenever I woke up, I'd find him reading *Steppenwolf*, smoking and drinking coffee. "How's it going, princess?"

Some people move through space with a certain subtlety. They look comfortable. You can tell that they showed up well-equipped for life and that everything's going to turn out fine for them. It's a striking sort of light. That's what Leo was like, with his university and his little house on the paramo. Though the lack of chemistry had always been mutual, something changed; we saw each other in a new way during that trip. That's how it works sometimes: a certain light shines on you and makes you look different. And it makes you look at other people in a particular way, too. The night we played Rummikub, as we both drank wine from the same clay cup we'd drink coffee from the next morning, as he told us all about his plans in Pakistan, he started to brush his hand across my hair and back, and eventually he drew me in from the waist as if that were a normal thing, sitting me down in his lap as if he knew what I liked. After a while we stood up and went to his room. The others stayed, shuffling cards. It was cold. We woke up in each other's arms. I moved in with him for the last few days, and I said goodbye to him in the bus station with sorrow and rage, a bad taste in my mouth, a sense of foreboding. In Caracas the next day, just after I'd gotten home, the phone rang.

"We're very close. I can smell you."

Fuck.

"I'm waiting for you," he added.

I searched the house for the car keys. He couldn't know. It couldn't be that he already knew. My legs shook. I emptied my purse, went into the kitchen, returned to the living room, lifted the sofa cushions, frantic, hoping desperately that this appearance was sheer chance: don't come looking for me and don't call me, because people come back when it's time. Everyone comes back, Rafael often told me. *Todos vuelven.* Everyone comes back. I dug through the mountain that had newly emerged from my bag. Walking out the front door, I felt the polished cement under my feet. I turned around and went back in. I put on my shoes and lost the keys again. What goes around comes around, he'd also say.

What does, goddammit? And where does it come to?

It was too much of a coincidence. He had to know. But who? Caboose? I never found out. I retraced my steps. I finally found the keys in my pants pocket. I sat down on the couch. I looked at myself in the bathroom mirror. And I stayed there, suspended. I don't know much time passed before I walked out the door again. I drove off toward Las Tres Gracias. It wasn't like I could leave him there forever, waiting on the bench at the bus stop.

To recognize each other, to relearn how to trust each other. To have someone. To go backwards and find missing steps without the certainty of wanting to follow them again. To wonder what to do and how to act before answering the question yourself.

A clay-colored man was waiting for me, thick-bearded, gaunt, in the usual place. His hair extended below his shoulders. I followed the roundabout. I sped up. He vanished from the rear-view mirror. In the reflection, what I saw was the daguerreotype of Red Rocks. That night I slept in the clinic. The next morning, early, I went straight to train. When I came home to shower and carry on with the day, I found him in the doorway. Same clothes from the day before, same color. The same smell as always. He was drinking a coffee from the corner bakery. He took my face into his hands, hard, and gave me the most delicate kiss, his tongue like dense jam. He slipped his hand under my shirt. He never asked: can I, is it okay if I put my hand here. He never asked. He'd just make his way, sometimes slowly. Never pausing.

"Bird. I waited for you."

A cat walked down the street. I knew it was a female cat because its markings were three different colors. She sat on the sidewalk, licking her front paws. I wanted to scream, and at the same time I didn't know what I'd be saying if I did, what I'd be screaming for. I wanted to cry but I just stared at the cat. She was licking her haunches now. Three-color cats are always female.

"I've totally mastered the technique now. You have to see me do it. It's fucking incredible to have wings, to soar like that." After a silence, he added, tilting his head, his brow creasing a bit, his words leisurely and precise: "The old wings broke."

I felt my cells contract. The precipice. The shrinking of all possibilities. The dark.

"But let's not talk about that now. Look. I need you to give me a ride tomorrow night and then to come get me again the next morning."

"I don't know. I have to be with my mom. I usually sleep there."

People don't disappear overnight, although some like to think so. We build our own landing strips. Our nests. I thought of Leo, probably somewhere in the clouds on his way to Pakistan by then, and I wondered if he'd remember me. I wondered how many women Rafael had slept with since the last time. It doesn't matter. Lots of sex, not much sex. It doesn't matter.

"Do you want to take a shower? Do you have clean clothes? You can rest while I do some stuff." Some stuff.

"I'll come with you," he said, running his fingers through his hair, pulling at his shirt as if smoothing it out with his hands would make it clean.

"No, really. You don't have to. Just relax here. Rinse off."

"Not even my mom knows I'm back."

"Call her."

"I'd better wait till after Parque Central. Just in case I crash and die," he said, half-laughing and half-serious. "It would be pretty fucked up to call and say hi and then kick the bucket the next day. Don't you think?"

"I'll be right back. Take a rest. Sleep."

We went in. I gave him a towel, a tightly rolled joint to help him unwind.

"You've really hardened up, haven't you?" he asked, pinching my ass. "Lots of training, huh? I heard you went to Mérida." He grabbed my thighs, his hands like pliers, and concluded without waiting me to respond: "You're stronger."

I glanced at the clock. "I'm running late."

We planned things out later with a pack of beers in the freezer and the team in my kitchen. Since my mom wasn't home, they stayed for several nights. I didn't care; I was sleeping at the clinic. Carlos—totally uninformed, as usual; on the moon—apparently called one night. No one managed to tell me about it.

"What do you think you're doing?" he asked me the next day in the hall of the clinic.

"I don't know. You tell me. You tell me what I'm doing."

"If you don't want to sleep alone"—on the moon!—"then come with us. You can spend the night whenever you want. Your siblings would be happy," he said after a pause. "They'd be happy to have you there."

"'Your siblings would be happy.' Of course."

There's no climber alive who doesn't know how to make a good pot of lentils, or some baked plantains, who doesn't know how to sweep and mop. When you're a guest in someone's house, you go to the grocery store and cook for your hosts, no questions asked. You help out however you can and otherwise make yourself invisible. A cut of beef, some fried eggs, anything. You run errands, take their kids to school, play the babysitter. When you take off, you leave everything as you found it, or better, so everyone's happy and grateful. If we went from hotel to hotel, we wouldn't make it as far as the corner. It's a network. You scratch my back, I scratch yours.

I'd walk into the house and find them lying on the couch, shoes off, feet up on the table, with an open beer and the TV on. The house: immaculate. Clean laundry. Folded, even. Hot food and company to eat it. A joint, good conversation. I was sleeping so poorly at the clinic that I'd nod off at strange hours, always aware that the world carried on in the living room, that there was someone else doing things when I disengaged. A rope connecting me to earth. I'd wake very early and try not to make noise, try not to wake them.

This was the plan. Rafael would go to Parque Central on his own at five-thirty in the afternoon, dressed in civilian clothes, a small backpack in tow. He'd go up the elevator in the eastern tower. He told me later that, when the doors opened on the twenty-third floor, he walked down an empty hallway and climbed up twenty more flights of stairs until he reached a level without a ceiling, full of debris, unlit. There had been a fire years before, and the site hadn't been much altered since. In my country, things fall apart un-mourned. Rafael spent the night in the abandoned supply room, forty-something stories in the air, in one of Caracas's most important government buildings. My job was to drive to Bolívar Avenue and wait for him with the engine running, ready to step on the gas when he landed, as soon as the sun was up. One miscalculation and Rafael would end up in jail—which is the same thing as beaten to a pulp in a holding cell. Either he'd go wild or the police would. That's how it would go. Or better put: he'd be fucked. No matter what, it would be a surefire way to get the shit beaten out of him.

The hardest part was stopping the cars along the boulevard; the few cars on the road at that hour were hurtling by. These days, no one drives at night at all. In my city, you're either erased by violence or by the fear of violence. There are fewer and fewer people in the streets. If things belong to those who use them, as Tomás says, Caracas now belongs to the criminals. Residents use it only for the bare minimum: for their survival. To put bread on the table, to earn enough *reales* to get through the day. At night, they stay in. If anything happened to them, that bread would go stale, uneaten. All the effort would be pointless. They live in terror. As for me, well, the night can find me where it finds me. For fuck's sake. If you're going to die, you're going to die. End of story.

Tomás was the transit operator: he'd carry a whistle and gesture gravely. I'd be waiting with the video camera aimed at the tower without knowing where I'd have to zoom in. I imagined the ritual with the comet, the dance, the utterance of the secret and incomprehensible phrase I'd heard at the Berkeley electrical tower. A hand emerged from an open window. First came the hand, then the rest of his body at the edge of the window. Knees flexed. The leap. The tiny form extended in the shape of a star. Three pedestrians, a beggar, and a night watchman applauded our commando operation, looking skyward, a star surrounded by mauve, growing larger with every second. An orange rectangle.

When he landed, he gathered everything up into a single knot and ran toward the SUV.

"Brrr, that was fucking terrifying. Step on it." And he added, changing his shirt: "Since five p.m. I've had three beers and two of your brownies. They were incredible." He reached out a hand to me. "And now I'll have one of these little thighs."

I left them celebrating and went to the clinic.

"You'll see. I'll cross to the other side and wait for you. I bet you'll show up there sooner than you think."

"Mom."

"I understand the thing about Carlos. I get that you don't want to stay at his house. I understand that. But the fact that he of all people is the one to tell me those good-for-nothings are living *in my house!*" she said, raising her voice at the phrase—"That's the last straw! I'm not going tolerate this, young lady."

She started to cough, but she continued. "In other words, while I'm over here dying, you're taking charge, throwing parties in my house. If you have to live alone, then you have to live alone, young lady. Because those vagrants are not setting a foot back into my house. Are we clear?"

"It's not what you think it is."

"I don't know what it is and I don't care. You're going to get them out of there and that's that. I can't believe you'd be so brainless. Or am I going to have to leave this place and take care of you like a baby?"

I apologized and said she was right. I said yes to everything. I asked them to leave. And they left. The rumors started in La Guairita; he disappeared for days. That he was lost to drugs and booze and women. That he was in jail. That he'd gone off on a trip. That he was in La Gran Sabana. That the Colombian girl was in Caracas.

That part was true, and while it provided him with an effective alibi, in the end it had nothing to do with his new disappearing acts.

"No way, Juli. That girl wouldn't want to see his face again even if it was in a painting," Lupe declared one day. "She says he's an asshole."

One afternoon I found him climbing the traverse in leather shoes, dress pants, and a bloodstained white shirt tied around his waist. He trailed an acidic, too-sweet stench behind him. He scaled several meters before he saw me. The rock's orange reflection made it hard to look at him directly.

"Bird! I love you!"

"Shit, Rafa, finally!"

"Finally what? Don't tell me you've missed me, have you? You don't miss anyone! A guy just turns his head for a minute and… what would Julia say if I asked her to marry me?" And he laughed. He started to blow me kisses with one hand. Hanging from a single arm. "Hey, Julia, what's it gonna be?" he asked, releasing his grip a little further, kicking as if he were about to fall. "Yes or no? I bet you're going to say no. You're such a tease," he said. Clowning. "But you'll never get married." Rocks tumbled down from up above, vulture feathers, dry leaves.

"Stop being so stupid. Get down! Get down from there!" I called. "Come on, don't be a baby."

"Ohhhh, I see. Not happening, girl. Go fuck whoever you want, go straight to hell with any fucking guy from Mérida. But don't you dare insult me. Whatever happens if you do, it won't be my fault."

"Get down from there right now. You're drunk, that's what you are."

"Don't you know that nobody fucks with me? You sure as hell know that nobody fucks with me," he shouted, laughing. I think he was laughing.

Despite the grit that stung my eyes every time I tried to look up, I could make out a wound on his right cheek.

"Go off and climb, Bird," he said in the end, his voice changing. "Stay down there. Far away. Because you're fucking pissing me off and I can't promise what will happen now. Make good use of your time while you've got it—don't you have a sick mom and a thesis to finish?"

I kept climbing up toward him, but he insisted: "Listen to me, Bird, I'm serious," he yelled. "You stay down there. You stay in one piece."

When you know, you know.

"Get out of here, love. Let's not fuck everything up all over again," he said, his tone softening before he vanished into the leaves like a sloth. A little deeper in, I heard him shout-singing *La calle es una selva de cemento, y de fieras salvajes...donde quiera te espera lo peor*—the street is a concrete jungle, full of wild animals...the worst is always lying in wait.

I got into the car, my face encrusted with dirt, chalk dust, and tears. I stared at myself in the mirror. I looked like a raccoon.

I asked everyone not to tell me anything. I'd leave the clinic at first light and go climbing as soon as the park opened. I lived in fear that he would turn up dead. Not because of a forced landing or faulty wings, not anymore, but because of a traffic accident, a fight in the street. I lived in fear that he would turn up alive. Period. The idea that I could run into him around a curve on the traverse, that I'd find him on my doorstep one morning like I once had, that he'd ring my buzzer in the middle of the night and I'd be there alone—it all terrified me. The waves of nausea worsened. Lupe would sleep over two or three nights a week. I spent the rest of my time at the clinic. I went to keep my mother company; I went so she'd keep me company. The idea that he'd gotten into a brawl at so-and-so's party. That he buys a six-pack every morning. That he climbs at night, and in leather shoes. That he's in jail and his mom said she won't bail him out anymore. That she's bailed him out. She called me one morning.

"He's been hit by a car. He was on his bike—you know how bad that road is. My baby's been hit. He says he wants to see you."

During those days in La Travesía, I found, in total, three red roses, two chrysanthemums, a teddy bear, two Baci chocolates. And, one afternoon, a shoebox on the roof of a car. With holes punched into the sides and the lid and a red rubber band.

"It looks like a toy. It's so clean," she said when I showed her a photo. "Are you sure you found it in the street, Julia?"

"Of course, Mom."

"Did you take it to the vet for its shots? It's not vaccinated if you found it in the street. Did you find it in the street?"

"Yes, Mom. That's what I'm telling you. In the street. And I got her vaccinated."

"So who put that little string around its neck?"

"I did! Who else? It's a female cat. She's a she."

The cat became a favorite topic of conversation. It wasn't bad at all, really, to worry about things other than her hair falling out and the chemo not working and her vomiting spells. Yes, I already told you that the shrubs are fine. No, she's not sharpening her claws on the couch. No, she doesn't pee anywhere other than her litter box.

"So he just showed up out of nowhere. Right in front of the house."

"Out of nowhere. Right in front of the house. And it's a she."

"Didn't you tell me it was in the street?"

"Fine, Mom, yes. In the street in front of the house."

"How's your child behaving?" she'd ask me as soon as I came into the room. "Aren't you going to give it a name? What happens when we're not home? Who's going to take care of it? Because I don't think I'll make it home again. And you're never there anyway, are you? If it were up to you, the poor thing would starve to death. I mean, you can't even take care of yourself," she'd say, laughing. She loved talking about it.

"You're not going anywhere, Mom. You set out some food in the morning and again at night. And she looks after herself during the day. Cats are like that. They don't need people to do much. They don't even like it if you do."

"And to think that your derelict boyfriend calls you Bird," she said to me one day, laughing. "You can tell he doesn't know you one bit. Bird! Yeah, right! Ha! Did you name the cat yet?"

"Yes."

"What's its name?"

"Bird."

"What?"

Things changed in the woods. I was the one who made the plans. Whenever I received a gift, I'd leave him a note with a date and time, a meeting place. Synchronicity. Sector B. Traca Traca. La Cueva del Bautizo. We'd leap at each other as soon as we were together.

"You can't tell anyone," I warned him, dressing afterward. "And don't call me. There's no need for that."

"You're going to drive me crazy, Bird."

One afternoon I found a note on the windshield: If you're going to come back, you have to leave first. Take care of your mom and don't worry, everything's going to be fine. Wait 4 me.

Five or six weeks later, there was no doubt about it. Not a single message, not a letter, nothing. Even Bird went missing. Rafa was gone. Or in jail again.

I went to his house.

"Oh, sweetheart, what can I say? He got some idea into his head—you know how he is. He showed up with a ticket to India, can you imagine? India! He sold the Jeep, it seems. That's what I was told, that he sold it. But who would ever buy that rattletrap, honey?"

"India?"

"He really didn't call you? Well, I just don't know," she said, shaking her head and fixing her eyes on the floor. "He said New Delhi was the door. He said that! But it's just as possible that he'll show up again three days from now, and it'll turn out that he's been driving that rickety old car all the way to Brazil."

Rafael's mother kept speaking without looking at me, talking to herself, rambling.

"I always said he shouldn't have bought it in the first place. That's what I told his father many times, that he shouldn't let him buy it," she said finally, wiping her eyes.

When people don't want to know, that's what they do: they blame objects. A Jeep. A pair of wings. Or the absence of certain objects. I couldn't call you because there was no phone. The post office was miles away. You blame the objects and you're all set.

"Help me, honey. Let's see. What do you think? Where could he have run off to?"

The smoke signals disappeared, the phone calls that cut off before I could speak; I stopped receiving messages from strangers. Fabi didn't know and neither did Lupe. The Colombian girl was still in Caracas, and the look on her face suggested she didn't know, either. I saw her in La Guairita all the time, wandering alone like a stray dog. Rafael had vanished, disintegrated. The parachute opens, the parachute explodes, Rafael turns to dust. Just like that. One false step and there's the precipice. Ravine. Plunge. Ten months passed. In ten months, you die, you're reborn, you die all over again. ⌗

Chapter XIII

The day it was announced that Pluto wasn't a planet, the phone rang.

"I am a friend who has something for you," a voice said in battered, musical Spanish, unmarked by anything that would help me guess where it came from.

"What? From Kathmandu?"

I suggested we meet in La Guacamaya, which would be busy, as it was every Saturday. The guy turned out to be a Brazilian with an unplaceable accent, part Iberian, part Colombian, part Mexican. Impossible to know where he'd learned the language. Everywhere, I guess. I didn't ask. He smelled of sweat and sun. He barely knew Rafael and had no idea where he was. He gave me the sandalwood Hanuman and a photograph of myself with a message scrawled on the back: *I could stop a moving train.*

"Now, I do not know. I used to see him at Smoke. Almost every night," he said, exposing a set of yellowed teeth in a short-lived smile. I didn't answer. He wore a silver-plated ring on every finger of his right hand. Entwined snakes. An elephant. Thorns. A sun with a moon inside. His fingernails were dirty. As if propelled by a spring, he lifted his pack to his back and said goodbye.

"Good luck with the jump," he said, gesturing to the Hanuman with a slight shift of his head and lips.

"The jump?"

"I hope you will find him," he added, though I hadn't said anything about looking for anyone. He disappeared as quickly as he had come, zigzagging, dark and agile, like a thief among the passengers, and vanished into the mouth of the subway. I stood there with the photo in one hand and the carving in the other, absorbing the noise around me and wondering why he couldn't have used a fucking piece of paper—a dirty napkin, for Christ's sake—to write down the goddamn message without having to return the photo of me. I came back to earth when one of the waiters, wearing a bow tie and polyester jacket, bumped into me with a tray and spilled a watermelon smoothie all over my shirt.

Two weeks later, I got a package in the mail.

A letter's content depends on the context of its reception, the mood you're in when you open the envelope. That afternoon, I didn't wait. I sat down on the floor. The sender was false. The recipient's name: Bird. And last name: de la Guairita. Then my address. I pulled off the lid. Inside was a DVD with an inscription in red marker—"Here, take my wings"—and a piece of paper with the OM symbol full of birds, suns, lizards, and mountains on one side. On the other was the phrase "I love you" penned up and down the margins, and in the center were two words and a number, the classic message, *Wait 4 me*. There was also a sticker of a monkey just like the carving, but this one was hanging in the air with its legs open like a pair of scissors, flying over a mountain. Within a couple days, he called home, left a message saying that he was coming back.

"I'll be there tomorrow, Mom."

Three weeks passed. It doesn't take long. People need just a few days to fall in love and change their plans, travel far away and come home again, get sick and get well, get sick and die. A few weeks can mean oblivion, an excursion, a cliff, a leap, a prison. An ineffective course of chemotherapy.

"If anything happens to me, I want to be left on the mountain," Rafael would sometimes say when he'd had too much to drink or had nothing else to say. A manifesto proclaimed in the middle of an alcohol-soaked night, or in a moment of consuming idleness and boredom: "It's expensive to get a body down. And there isn't much left after the final splat, is there, Bird? Ever seen a dead body get out of bed and tell you something?"

"If it's easy enough, I want to be cremated," I responded once, when my mom's situation wasn't looking good.

"I want to be left wherever I split open, end of story," he said. "I'm not going to torture anyone like that. Just think of Fabi's cousin. Two years with her dad in a little urn in her living room. With his photo next to it. Two years wondering whether to leave him on the Pico Oriental or the Pico Occidental. Whether she should toss him off one of the peaks or from some random tree. Whether to carve something into the bark or plant him there, ta-da, under the random tree."

"Shit, of *course*! It'd be so much better to smash into the ground! Better to go out in a flash than die a slow death," I snapped, angry. "If you're going to die no matter what, then just die already," I finished, shooting him a furious look, though I already felt guilty about my reaction, for what was both a retort and a wish. Die, motherfucker, I was telling him. I know I can't count on you, is what I also meant. I know I can't count on you even if I'm dead, is what I wanted him to understand. But what I actually said aloud was: "My point is that if you die in a comfortable spot, it's better to be cremated. Right?"

A comfortable spot. I said that.

"But the thing is it's better to die in the mountains. That whole thing about dying in the hospital, nothing's worse than that. I'm going to die in the mountains or by falling off one. It doesn't matter as long as it's far away."

"Let the people who are left behind decide, not the person who dies," I concluded. "If you don't have anyone to bury or cremate you, better leave it to chance."

"What matters isn't the one who left but the one who's on his way, sweetheart," my mom would say whenever Rafael disappeared. "New life. Even though it wasn't your decision, make the most of it. People don't always have the strength to decide. But you can accept."

When her pain grew constant and she stopped eating, the doctor said they would start giving her morphine, that we should let the nurses know when she was uncomfortable. For a moment I thought this was good news. No more middle-of-the-night moans. At last, more nights of uninterrupted sleep. Finally, a truce. But it quickly dawned on me that we weren't leaving the clinic.

"If there's anything you need to tell her, anything you want to organize, now would be a good time for you to do that," said the doctor. "The next phase is going to be difficult."

I stopped holding on to my mother to make her stay, and I started getting ready. She was choking more often. She was receiving injections to stop the hallucinations. Carlos appeared sometime around then with a Buddhist book on the importance of letting go mindfully, calmly, conscious of what's coming, of how to say goodbye and leave your affairs in order. *The Great Book of Natural Liberation through Understanding in the Between.* Jesus.

On the last night, my mom was struggling to breathe. I remember her barely lit by the dim lamp embedded in the headboard. I was sitting in an armchair, leaning my forehead onto the mattress, holding her hand, newly freed of its needles, and trying to rest. She let out a sound and I lifted my face. I stroked her forehead. She opened her eyes for the first time in hours. And so I talked to her about her life, about myself and how happy I was to have had her as my mother, made a joke or two: "Look at what a good job you did with me." I talked to her about Carlos: "We never needed him, you see? You were right. You're reversible: mom on one side, dad on the other."

I told her how brave she was, that she was an example to follow, and I told her other things: how strong she'd been throughout her illness, how hard she'd fought. "You know I'm strong, too, right? I love you very much, Mommy." Her eyes were closed. Two tears slid down. Maybe she was crying, maybe it was a reflex. Who can say. "Mom. I'm here, Mom. I'm talking to you, can you hear me? Are you listening to me? It's me, Julia."

She started to choke again. To cough. She vomited. I ran out to call the nurse. I was shouting in the hall, wiping my eyes. Three nurses came in, did nothing, and left the room again. I fell asleep thinking of the Radiant Light. Her moans woke me again.

"Hail Mary, full of grace," I began, wondering how much of the prayer I'd remember. The verses revealed themselves one by one. It's incredible how many things you know without knowing you know them. The number of things you don't forget. But the problem is you shed one tear and then it's impossible to hold back the rest, so I had to stop praying anyway. She opened her eyes. When I noticed, I found her looking at me as if she'd just woken from a nap and discovered a stranger sitting beside her. She wheezed, gasped, went rigid, let out a noise, exhaled. Whatever was left, it vanished with this fragile thread of air. What had she thought when she looked at me, opening her eyes for the last time?

I sat on the couch until Carlos arrived. He took care of everything. Someone in the house had made a pot of soup that neither of us tasted. We cried quietly, mourning as you mourn people who die painful deaths, transformed into remains. I couldn't sleep, so I went to the Pico Naiguatá as soon as the sun started to rise, bringing a cold *arepa*, a piece of raw cane sugar, and three tangerines in my backpack. I thought about comfortable deaths. About comfortable spots to die.

I didn't go to the wake or the funeral. I walked back into the house three days later with an intensified fear of treading harder than I had to, of breaking something, of a drawer or a closet door swinging open. I was afraid that the house would decide to talk to me, to tell me who knows what. The figures in every photograph seemed to turn their backs to avoid my eyes, or else they stared out at me with the same dazed expression as my mother's on the last night. The Buddhist book about death, which I'd left on the dining room table, was gone. Bird had come back and I held her in my arms, weeping. "Your name's going to be Grigrí," I told her. And then I repeated it into the air: "Mom, the kitty came back and her name is going to be Grigrí."

Carlos helped me with the paperwork and loaned me money. One thousand eight hundred dollars and the ticket. Enough to get started. Sometimes I think they were two sides of the same coin; that it was true—she had to disappear for him to be there. He denies it. He says everything happens in its own time, that God's time is perfect. That he'd always been there. God's time is perfect, huh, asshole? I feel like asking him. But I don't, mostly because I'm light years away. 🈺

CHAPTER XIV

I've never minded waiting for hours at the gate, or the cold sandwiches, or the ache in my shoulders from heavy luggage. I like airports—their sleepless nights, their curt language. Their races and their parentheses around nothing. Their emptinesses. I like missing flights and sprinting to make them. I like categorizing travelers' faces by their expressions, and I like staring out the window at that critical landscape: the entomological scale of the mechanics and drivers, with their tiny trucks transporting colorful rectangles onto the conveyor belts and into the planes. And then comes the part I find impossible to believe (I'm no bird, that's for sure): the titanic body rising up like a dandelion.

As for train stations, I love the movement, the people flocking from one door to the next, from one line to the next, depending on which train is departing for where. All night long. You can sit in the waiting rooms beside the people who are about to leave. They sit right there next to you, eating something, drinking coffee, but they're really already gone. When there aren't any glass barriers or customs inspections, you grip the handrail on the steps to the train car, heave your luggage upward, ascend a stair or two, and slip into another time. You're already gone. You take three steps back and there you stay. You can change your mind. I love the clatter of the wheels on the platform. The metallic rhythm, the way its departure is both a sound and a gradual pulse. In an airport, all noise from the outside world is hidden. Everything is cleaner, but who says you travel to be clean. In an airport, you have to know where you're going, or at least look the part. If you want to go back out, you have to ask permission; you seem suspicious if you suddenly change your mind. Your sovereignty over your own body is farther out of reach. It's better to travel without so much paperwork, closer to the body itself.

I landed in the Delhi airport on March 18. My backpack took some time to appear. I'd brought the DVD; the photo from that day in Parque Central; a photo of my mom on her second-to-last birthday—she must have already been sick by then; the teddy bear from La Travesía; a photo of Grigri; and the crystal from Roraima. "Knickknacks, honey, that's all they are. You settle for knickknacks," she'd say when I'd show her Rafael's gifts toward the beginning. In the backpack I'd brought my gear, three pairs of climbing shoes, one pair of ice climbing boots, and another pair of trekking boots. Running shoes, a bathing suit, and my mother's flip-flops. "Don't get into those showers without anything on your feet. Who knows how filthy they'll be." The bathing suit was my own hang-up. You never know where you'll end up showering or with who.

Between the jetlag and the exhaustion of spending over a full day in planes and airports, I was completely blank. I like to think that only your body survives when you travel; it's the only witness. Everything else disintegrates, luckily. By the time you're done, you're no longer who you were. There's just a photo album in a box. Or a DVD that stays on pause until you hit play again. In the end, you're someone else.

Sometimes I'd put on my parachute: you don't know if he wants you to find him, you don't know how he is or who he's with. The only thing that matters is that you see him and get out of all this.

140

Maybe he died, maybe he doesn't want to see you. Whatever it is, let it be, I'd repeat to myself. Whatever happens, happens. Communication in the mountains is always the same, I'd tell myself. It's always easier. You're more likely to find him in the Himalayas than on the street or in a jail or a hospital in Pakistan or India. As soon as I got to the airport, I resolved to follow the trails of coincidences wherever they took me, but I desperately hoped they'd lead me into the mountains; I asked my mother to lead me away from the city and toward a mountain. And since at that point my only information had come from the Brazilian guy, it didn't even matter where I started. As I waited at the baggage claim, I also waited for something or someone to speak to me.

"Coincidence? Come on. There's no such thing as coincidence. Everything is *causal*, not casual," says Tomás. "Cau-sality." He's just like Carlos.

A skinny man walked past me, barefoot. His feet were black, split, swollen. I imagined his soles tough as leather. I wondered how long I'd stay on this side of the globe. The feet of everyone else around me looked equally battered. I thought of my mother, saw her covering her face with her hands, shaking her head, complaining about the uncleanliness, the smells. If you travel in sandals around an entire continent crisscrossed with badly paved highways or just dirt roads, Mom, how would *your* feet end up? It doesn't mean he's dirty, I imagined myself telling her. I've never broken the habit of fighting with her.

Planning the trip in Caracas, I'd booked a room at a hotel that seemed—from the website, at least—like a good base camp. Dear Miss Julia. Thank you for your email. We are pleased to confirm your place on the free shuttle from the airport to the hotel and from the hotel to the airport, which we offer twenty-four hours a day, seven days a week. There is no need to make an online reservation. Send us your flight number and we will make a reservation on your behalf. Please contact us for any further information or additional assistance. With best wishes, G. P. Singh. General Manager – Best Imperial Hotels.

The exit looked like an abandoned parking lot. There were five uniformed men waiting there, holding signs that announced the names of various passengers. One of them handed me a card I folded and dropped into a flowerpot when he wasn't looking. I sat down on a bench and hid behind my travel notebook to forget the time and furtively observe the scene. It's always good to look busy. The automatic doors opened less and less often. Outside was a dim expanse of ground that grew increasingly hazy as I tried to identify details. A grainy, blown-up sepia photo. I took two or three blurry pictures before putting my camera away. You're pushing it, little Bird.

I can't remember if I introduced myself to the driver. He was supposedly from the hotel. He lifted my pack onto his head and carried it toward the car, balancing there, not touching it. In the mealy darkness, I imagined lurching ahead to snatch my luggage and run back into the airport; I thought of how ridiculous it would look. I imagined the men at the entrance laughing at me. Better dead than drenched in blood—dignity at all costs. If this is how it it's going to end, then how absurd, I thought. I didn't care. The man didn't know how to drive. It took him twenty maneuvers to ease out of his parking space, and the precariousness reassured me somehow. It would make sense for me to die now, I thought anyway. Without achieving anything. Running away. Yes. That would be causality, Tomás. My fear dissolved. Death is just the worst-case scenario.

I'm almost certain that the hotel was just three or four streets away from the airport but that we went in circles around the same few blocks before parking. It took forty minutes to get there. It was a medium-sized building. We walked through the glass front door and its aluminum jambs. As we passed through, I heard the clinking of the bells hung from the doorframe. The lobby had two small worn-out couches, the front desk, and a TV affixed to the wall, which was showing a basketball game. One of the three men in rubber sandals and rolled-up pants got up and went to the cubbyholes, dragging his half-shod feet. He pulled out a key labeled with the number 27.

I paid forty dollars, a fortune, and another man took me upstairs in an elevator with metal sliding grates that looked like it was designed for cargo. Three floors. There was only light inside the elevator box. Staring out through the grates and into the darkness, the whole place looked abandoned, its hallways endlessly long. The elevator rattled and banged to a halt, the man hauled open the door with a screech, and he motioned me through, leading me down the corridor. I nearly stumbled into a shadow stretched out on the floor from wall to wall. I thought it was some drunk guy unable to crown the night in his own room.

"If you have any trouble, you may tell the watchman. He's here all night," said my guide, gesturing down toward the man as we stepped over him. On the floor, to his right, was a *tali* with some uneaten food.

It's bad news if there's a man guarding every hall, I thought, and if he's asleep, well, that's worse. We entered the room. The first thing I did was confirm that the door had a lock. While my host showed me the bed, the TV, the location of the light switches, and tried to show me the bathroom, I stayed firmly rooted in the doorway, saying yes to everything. Wonderful, perfect, thank you. When he said goodbye and left, I sat down on the edge of the bed. I sniffed the shabby bedspread, brushed a hand down the walls.

I went into the bathroom. I opened the shower curtain to make sure no one else was there. A cockroach. I wanted to throw a boot at it, but I was too slow; by the time I'd managed to undo the knots keeping the boots in place, it had already fled down the drain. I turned on the TV. The channels were all in Hindi. I watched a soap opera for a while. A couple kissing: she'd dry her eyes, he'd take her hands into his and say something to her, and just like that—no anesthesia—they'd burst into song, accompanied by a ballet troupe that seemed, bafflingly, to come out of nowhere. I switched off the TV in case anything was happening outside. I scanned the room for water. There was a small bottle I finished in three gulps. I re-checked the locks, trying not to make noise, hoping the man who was supposed to look after me wouldn't discover I was there.

I pulled out my travel notebook and the bear and sat down on the bed. The day I found the teddy bear in one of the caves, I almost slipped and fell. The little creature had a map with a date and time hanging around his neck. I thought of that afternoon and registered how tired my body was. Caracas time was so far away. I wondered whether the device that Carlos had installed to turn the house lights on and off would work. That was the sort of thing my mother couldn't stand. "He's like a child," she'd say. "He loves his little gadgets. It's all a game to him. That's all he cares about, his little toys."

I wondered if Mariela would water the plants.

I didn't move, strangulating the teddy bear, staring at the door, thinking of how appalled my mother would be if she could see me there. I stood and bolted for the bathroom. I threw up.

"Julia has what it takes," I heard her tell Carlos in the doorway one night. That's where all of their conversations happened, on the dividing line between the vestibule and the street. Between the family and the world. "Julia has what it takes. Don't worry, she's like me. She'll leave that bum in a second."

Sinking back down onto the faded bedspread, I chose not to cry out of consideration for her. Crying, I felt, would mean bothering her for no reason. I fell asleep on the edge of the bed, which actually just smelled like soap. The phone rang at four. "Good morning, madam. The taxi is waiting for you in the lobby. *Namaste.*"

I appeared downstairs exactly as I'd come: wearing the same clothes, unshowered. I don't know if I thanked the man at the front desk, but I don't think so. 五

Chapter XV

Light changes everything. I arrived at a very modern airport that teemed with people. I looked at their phones and computers from afar. The visa line was endless, so I spent some time surveying the landscape I found both so familiar and so strange. On my way out, I took a map from a tourist information booth and the clerk helped me find an area, a hostel, and an eco/adventure travel agency. I made two local calls. Despite myself, I felt like just another tourist.

The color and mood of Kathmandu is how you'd imagine the color and mood of Kathmandu. In the late afternoon, the landscape seems filtered through orange cellophane. At dawn, ochre and smoky gray. The houses and other structures look like building blocks, one on top of the other, chaotic, or one right next to the other without any paths or sidewalks separating them. Only the façades are painted. They're gray on both sides, and sometimes the view deceives you into thinking they're under construction, but then you take in the context and you realize they're not. Like I said, they're painted only across the front-facing sides. Some urban beautification policy left them this way, like façades on a theater set. Electrical cables tangle between buildings like spider webs. The Luna turned out to be a small, clean, normal hotel. When I arrived, I was handed the key to room #63 and I went upstairs unaccompanied. After a shower, I sat down on the bed with the towel wrapped around my head to study the map and locate some of the major temples. I thought Rafael could easily appear in a couple of days and put an end to it all. Better make use of the time. Once the name KEEP appeared, hovering over the map, I set out to entertain myself with something else. I ended up reading a book at the front desk about the temples and other tourist sites. The usual recommendations: don't eat street food, don't drink water of dubious origins, try local ingredients little by little, don't take rickshaws in the middle of the night, wear long sleeves and scarves depending on the area. I didn't call Caracas. No one will notice two or three days of silence, I told myself.

Thamel is the touristy part. Ganja, hashish, massages, textile stores, pashmina shawls, Ganeshas, Buddhas, elephants of different materials and prices. Metal strainers, pipes, spoons, bells. Gas pumps, electric and kerosene lamps, lanterns, all as good as new. Nuts and dried fruit. Maps. Internet. *Looking for a hotel? Taxi, madam? Rickshaw!* Between stalls, heaps of mountaineering equipment for sale. All kinds: from stalls offering a jumble of boots, ripped jackets, and thermal clothes hung haphazardly on metal hangers alongside other ultra-technological ones still sealed in their packages, to stands where you can spend hours reading maps and hiring sherpas. The alleyways are filled with a mishmash of strange languages that turn out to be English. Sometimes you hear Devanagari. The voices vanish in the clatter of the rickshaws and the roar of motorcycles and their ear-splitting horns. You rarely see trashcans, and some sidewalks turn into garbage dumps collected in pick-up trucks every few days. When they take too long to show up, the neighbors burn the trash. It smells like plastic and charred meat. The first time I asked at the hotel and I was told no, it doesn't smell of meat, but I'm certain. It smells of flesh.

I was mesmerized by Kathmandu's symphonic disarray. It's hard to believe, but those streets have their own tempo, their own pauses. Caracas only wishes that its own chaos were so rhythmic.

I bought a mangosteen juice and then a starfruit juice with an impressively equipped cart: it had six or seven blenders and the fruit was arranged by size and color. I took some photos. The dragonfruits looked like heliconia blossoms. You travel so far to find this sort of thing: the flowers in your garden transformed into fruit. I walked, got lost, got un-lost, and ended the day sitting on the ground under many pounds of clothes and tapestries, drinking chai, hypnotized by the colors and textures that served as a blanket for me, or a ballast. Eventually I couldn't stand up under their weight. I bought an amethyst-colored pashmina shawl and emerged on the street, already feeling guilty for the unnecessary expense, the waste of time. As punishment, I made myself stop at KEEP. Even if it was just to figure out where it was. I stood at the corner for almost half an hour, watching people come and go. I ate a pizza on my way back to the hotel. When I reached it, I ran upstairs to vomit.

Waking up the next day, grazing against the clothes I'd left at the foot of the bed, I discovered the aromas of the city again. You spend the whole trip smelling of curry, cumin, cardamom. At first it's just your clothing, then it's your skin. You sweat curry without realizing it. That's how it is with everything. After a certain point, you're so overwhelmed by sensations that you stop feeling them. Otherwise you explode. That's how it is with everything. I couldn't put off KEEP forever, so I walked over and went in after breakfast.

A train at top speed crashing and echoing in my brain. Emptiness.

The walls were plastered with maps, topos of different routes, and autographed posters. Photos and notes from travelers covered two huge bulletin boards in the entrance like messy mosaics. Men and women sheathed in their mountaineering suits, surrounded by snow, their noses burned. Four Asian climbers with the Korean flag, flashing the peace sign with their fingers. Hikers celebrating in some bar, their skin peeling. The view from the summit of the Dhaulagiri massif. A photo of Mount Kailash: a perfect triangle.

Messages: "John, I'm trying to find you, you left your camera with my gear, get in touch," and a phone number. "Looking for volunteer to complete a climb up Meru Peak." Proper names of people, mountains, roads. Numbers: phone numbers, meters, kilometers, levels of difficulty. Climbing topos. Penned on paper of all different colors and sizes. Messages from climbers in their post-peak trances. Strange words. "NEVEREST." The business cards of taxi drivers, travel agencies, massage therapists, acupuncturists, and hotels across the country. I stared at the image of a seated man looking into the camera, his eyes like a tunnel, black and glittering as a pair of beetles. His body relaxed, slouched back into the sofa with the bottle in front of him like a sign, like proof: I didn't die, here I am.

"You have to look fear right in the eye, Julia. That's how it works: you see it and *poof*, it disappears. If you turn away, it'll eat you alive. Fear eats you alive if you don't look at it. So watch out."

I drew a little closer, made sure no one was looking, and tugged the photo off the board instead of taking a card or a note. My legs were shaking, and the sweat on my palms became a stream trickling down my neck and back. I tucked the photo into my coat pocket. Everything started to crumble, the snow on the summits began to melt, to disintegrate into avalanches of images, sentences, ideas. I imagined Rafael in the face of uncertainty, of the new.

"Julia, you can't see it, but we're the same, you and me. Don't you get it?"

From then on, I kept the stranger's photo in my pocket next to Rafael's. It became an adopted amulet. The B-side of Rafael.

And sometimes I'd picture him holding the photo in his hand, threatening me, demanding to know: "So who's this guy? Who the fuck is he, Bird?"

Chapter XVI

Being there, far from everything I'd left behind, including myself, I felt once again that we were animals from the same species. From the same puddle. He always seemed relieved, as if we were proving his theory when we kissed.

Two years before Kathmandu, there had been other little multicolored papers pinned to a bulletin board in another mountaineers' café. Ernesto and Andrés and I got to Lima on a May afternoon. I barely got to see the city, because that same night we found ourselves in a bus station where my fanny pack was stolen, with my CD player and CDs inside. In the time it took me to step toward Andrés and hand him my part of the ticket money, the fanny pack was gone. Until then, I'd always traveled with my musical selection on me. The luxury I'd trained for. Rafael did the same; he always packed his mix CDs. If you can carry them, why leave them behind.

At four in the morning the next day, and after over five hours on the highway, we reached Huaraz. A small town: I remember the women, their cheeks, heavy skirts, one wool sweater on top of the other, aprons, ponchos, multicoated as onions. "Layering," the gringos call it, as if they'd invented it all by themselves. The women of the Cordillera look like ragdolls and they're the queens of layering. I remember an open-air neighborhood market. And a street, probably the main street, with a dry-dirt traffic island and little bushes lined up down the middle. The landscape in the distance was triangular: dark brown, white, electric blue.

We easily found a double room for a dollar-fifty where we weren't going to be sleeping, anyway. All we needed was a place to store Ernesto's tent, which was very heavy in comparison to mine, and our city clothes. We hadn't brought much of those, but it's always overkill once you're up on the mountain, so we left them there in three plastic bags. We went out to the market, distributed the weight among our three packs, and made our way toward Cebollapampa by bus. Three thousand nine hundred thirty-five unforgettable meters. As soon as we arrived, we put on our packs and started walking, as if we were sick, as if we were my mother, as if the bank were about to close and the errand couldn't wait. An impending summit, stopwatches around our neck. We were like my mother. No one talked at all on that trip. I was eating a chocolate bar I'd bought in town as a special treat—the wrapper said "the best of the Andes"—and which turned out to be nothing special at all; little lumps of white sugar clustered inside. It was for making hot chocolate, I realized, studying the green and yellow paper more closely and noting that it also said in big letters: Corona. Stone-Ground Chocolate. For hot chocolate. The best of the Andes.

In a little under an hour, we approached and passed the first shelter. Four thousand six hundred eighty. The hikers lingered there. They mingled on the deck, looked out at the view, chatted, drank something steamy from a mug. Hot chocolate. The best of the Andes.

"What if we spent the night there to get acclimated?" I asked, conscious of how degrading my question was. You don't stay in the shelters. You never stay. Serious climbers don't fraternize with tourists. Only if they're paying you to.

"Five thousand two hundred isn't much," one of them said. "Don't worry."

"There's still a long way to go," the other said.

"If we start stopping now, we'll never get there."

They continued on mechanically. I lagged behind. For the first time in a long time, I was walking alone, and not because I'd chosen to. My legs were stiff as baseball bats, my shoulders slack, unable to hold my pack in place. The strap across my chest was bothering me. If I loosened it, the weight shifted unevenly and my back hurt. If I tightened it, it cut into my chest and I struggled to breathe. I cinched my hip-strap too close but didn't realize; I was so dazed that I didn't notice the sting and the scrapes until hours later. I sank toward the ground with every step. My head ached a little. They were out of sight in under two hours, but I didn't care; the path was obvious enough. When you're most tired is when you stop the least. You pay a heavy price for a five-second pause: your legs cramp, your kneecaps stiffen, you lose the rhythm of your breath. It hurts to start again. Stopping means going backwards.

When I reached the third hilltop, I called out to them. They looked tiny up above. I went faster on the descent, thinking I could reach them.

"Hey!"

Nothing.

"Heeeeeey!" I shouted louder.

"Motherfuckers!"

Nothing.

Minutes later, Ernesto stopped and looked behind him. Apathetically, he started to retrace his steps, eyes on the ground, kicking rocks.

"Are you okay? What's wrong?" He automatically lifted my load to his shoulders.

"Nothing. I feel weak in the legs. I have a headache," I started to say.

"Better not to talk. Breathe."

I quickened my step to keep from falling behind again. We reached Andrés. They unzipped my pack without a word. They pulled out food and cooking utensils first. Then my own gear. My underwear ended up scattered across the grass. The camera banged onto the ground and the lens cover slid off. Exchanging a couple syllables at most, not looking at me, they distributed almost everything between them. My hairbrush flew out and Andrés picked it up, testing the weight on his back.

"This thing really is heavy," he said, as if it were a crime. "Holy shit," he added with a cynical laugh. He left the brush on the ground.

"Let's go. You'll recover tonight," Ernesto said, tucking my camera into his pack.

"Don't keep stopping or you'll feel worse."

Before we set out again, I leaned forward to grab the brush. I wiped it clean on my shirt. Despite the lightness I'd just traded for humiliation, I walked on alone. I couldn't go any faster, but I didn't feel like looking around at the view, either. Taking in the landscape is a luxury I haven't always been able to afford. Another pressure cooker. I have no idea what that journey's like. After four hours of monologues and cursing, I made it to the campsite. Night had fallen. I was met by two headlamps around a kerosene stove, coca tea, mushroom risotto, and a pitched tent. I had to thank them.

"Tomorrow we're going to leave at three-thirty, really early. We don't want to waste any time."

"Take it easy till you feel better. We'll go up together in two days," Ernesto said, sketching in the dirt with a stick.

"Or we can wait and see," Andrés added.

"Rest, though," Ernesto concluded, and he brushed his hand across my head in an indifferent caress that felt more like a thwack. When I got to my feet, I looked down at Andrés's drawing. A peak in the shape of an ice cream cone and two climbers, joined together by a rope, ascending it. Below, in the cone part, a little dot. Another climber.

I turned and went into the tent. The backpack strap had scraped the skin off my waist. I pulled the sleeping bag up to my chin and cried. All that training just to get belittled by a pair of mountaineering executives. You don't show it when you're disappointed with yourself on the mountain. You don't fight with your climbing partners. You don't complain about the scrapes or the blows. These are things you don't do, especially if you're a woman and on your own. Then the rumors spread. *Sounds like Julia couldn't take it.* If you get mad, they say you're a bitch. If they see you cry, you're a baby. A few hours later, sunk deep in sleep, I heard them getting ready to leave. I pretended to be out cold. I wasn't interested; they looked bland to me, two eggs with no salt. It was good to sleep. To turn off my head. To stop seeing them altogether.

When the sun rose, I discovered we were camping on a white patch of a slope that culminated in a cliff. There wasn't much room to walk around. On the other side of the gorge, a wall was releasing avalanches. At first they sounded like thunder in the distance, but within seconds the noise was closer. I kept turning around; I couldn't get used to it. First the white powder in vertical free fall, a whistle. Then the cloud inflating and blurring at the edges, carrying more snow along the rock wall, making it hazy and white. Within seconds, everything returned to its usual precision. Then, a short time later, it repeated itself. Everything was silence—or, better put, everything was the wind in my ears, the cloth of the tent, the fire in the stove, until the avalanche came again. I spent the whole day in that eight-meter space, surrounded by infinity. The hours passed and I confirmed it again. I would have preferred it if no one had come back.

We reached the summit two days later. Six thousand three hundred ninety-five cloudless meters. The minimum amount of gear in our daypacks, relaxed lungs, strong thighs. We celebrated right there. We lay down in the snow and stayed there for a few moments like a happy family on any given Sunday at the Parque del Este in Caracas. We snapped a photo with each of our cameras. Much to my amazement, Andrés had been carrying a Venezuelan flag, which he took out. We can leave whenever, he said, after he'd taken his photo with the flag and returned it to his pack.

Once we'd returned to the campsite, I decided to head back on my own. Since we had only one tent, we were stuck with each other. I couldn't stay there alone and leave them without a tent, and I couldn't go tentless while they climbed, and I couldn't summit unaccompanied. There was nothing else to decide. I left them what they could use. I never saw them again. Not them, not the gear. They sent me a package from Bolivia months later. Four tools; the tent, ripped now; five socks, three of them mismatched. That same year, Andrés fell into a ravine on Kunturiri. He was an icicle by the time they got him out. I have no idea where Ernesto is; I've heard that he started surfing and grows aloe vera in Paria, but I really don't know.

In Huaraz, I mostly walked around, ate, and planned a trekking expedition. And in a pizzeria, right in front of the traditional wall lined with little brightly colored squares, a lot like the one I later saw in Kathmandu, I became aware of an English girl who was looking for company to trek up from the base. We met up the next day in the same spot. A few hours later, we were heading out with a porter. All those hills and black lagoons and emerald colors reminded me of how much I like trees and the color green, cooking on the mountain and not doing anything else, taking photos and finding something to take with me from everywhere I go. Once we were back, we went to Cuzco. After Macchu Picchu, she continued on by herself and I stayed for three more nights. That's where I met Ben. He did paragliding. He was a vegan. And Canadian. His body fit mine.

"I guess you always know when you're with the right person. Even your body knows," he told me after our first night together.

Traveling with a vegan isn't easy. When you finally find some beans, it turns out they have bacon or beef stock. Vegetables, pasta, mashed potatoes—they all have butter or cheese or both. Everything has egg in it, or refined sugar, or white flour. If you're not screwed one way, it's another. It's not easy. He reminded me of Tomás. Ben would eat plain spaghetti, parboiled potatoes, rice, and steamed vegetables, when there were any. Sick-person food to stay healthy. Otherwise, nuts and fruit. Three months later he appeared in Caracas and proposed to me. We had fun, but it's one thing to have fun and another to get married. Impossible. I hadn't even mentioned Rafael, so we went incognito to La Guairita—we snuck there, you could say—without him finding out. That's the last I heard from my future husband. We sent each other birthday cards for two years in a row and that was that. I never told Rafael about Ben, either. There was no reason to tell him.

In any case, if there was one thing I knew as I faced the bulletin boards at KEEP, in Kathmandu, it was that anything could happen when it came to changes-of-plans and those little scraps of paper, scrawled with stranger's names and handwriting and promises of adventure. Even the future husband who never was. It all depends on how willing you are to reach them, those paper squares, those plans, those people. ⽥

Chapter XVII

Against all expectations, Rafael had actually signed the guestbook at the store. When he'd climbed the Ávila, he'd appeared in the park rangers' log as José Luis Rodríguez, Mahatma Pérez, and John Long. I didn't think he'd do anything different in the Himalayas. But there was the handwriting I knew so well, jotted down beside a destination. He'd gone as a cook with a trekking team to the Everest base camp two weeks prior. Flipping back the pages, I found a trip he'd made to Trango, among others. The BASE jump was nowhere to be found.

"He's been here for two months," said the girl at the register when I asked her. "He hasn't come back from his last trip. And I don't think he will," she added, before grudgingly handing me a piece of paper: *Experience the thrill of skydiving over Mount Everest.* Beneath it was his name, and, of course, a photo of him making the peace sign. Tourists love V for Victory, he always says.

That's how I learned he was a regular climber on the local scene. That he had a job—or he'd had a job for a while, more like it—and although he hadn't returned from his last expedition, he was technically fired. He lived in Kathmandu; he wasn't passing through Kathmandu. He had no known climbing plans. He was just there, living. I learned more. That he'd gotten into several fights, that the mountain police force had found him after he'd jumped off Bhote Kose and nearly arrested him, but he was faster than they were. He left his parachute tangled on the ground and ran toward the edge of a cliff and no one dared to follow. He reappeared at KEEP three days later, with scratches all over his body and a bandaged wrist; he said he'd gotten lost on the mountain on his way back to the city. Every story sounded familiar to me. They all bore his signature, his childish scrawl. I was almost certain, besides, that at some point he'd slept with the bratty girl from the store. According to the KEEP crew, he wasn't in jail, though no one knew when he'd be back. That is, they knew he was traveling, but he never returned on the day he said he would, so it was hard to know. And this, too: that as soon as he showed up, he'd get kicked out. He wasn't drowning in a pool of alcohol, he wasn't sick. "You can go home now," I told myself. "Go home," I was telling myself, when the girl interrupted me.

"All we know is this," she told me with some reluctance. She must have thought I'd never leave her in peace if she just didn't come out with it. She pulled out the parachute, its cords jumbled together like a plate of spaghetti. "Someone tried to sell them to Jim in Thamel a couple days ago. A cop re-sold them and someone bought them and then tried to sell them, and you know," she said, "the usual. They ended up here, of all places. So near and yet so far and all that. Because if it were up to me, he'd never see them again. Take them, if you want," she finished, setting the wings on the counter. I bet he fucked her and then left her without so much as a backward glance.

I had basically the same routine every day. Wake up, run ten kilometers, go down for breakfast, go to KEEP, and if the girl wasn't at the store, visit Frontiers to chat with Graham, or go to The Last Resort. Have lunch at some point. Stop by the Rasta bar on the corner and finish the day at Smoke. Every other day, pull-ups and flexes: ten sets of ten. That was it. A daily visit to the internet café.

I was always assigned the same computer. The U, T, A, V, and K were rubbed off the keyboard. That's when I started paying attention. Everywhere. I have a collection of photos. It's always more or less the same letters that get erased.

"Julia, sweetheart, how are you? Where are you? You haven't written us for a while and we're worried. Please write. Your cousins ask after you and your brother and sister send you kisses. We're waiting for you. Grigri's gotten really big. I built a house for her, with a little door that opens to let her in. She still doesn't know how to use it, she still sleeps outside of the house, but she'll figure out the mechanism and get used to it anytime now."

She'll figure out the mechanism and get used to it anytime now, he said.

When the expedition team had been back for several days and Rafael still hadn't showed signs of life, Ram gave me a more detailed explanation. They'd sent him a message from the store. A sherpa brought it to him along with his load of oil, batteries, and garbage bags, and that must be why he hadn't come back.

"Why would he come back? So we can kick him out for real? At least you took the wings. I don't think we'll be seeing him around here anymore."

He'd come to blows with the group leader during the trip, and he'd also been caught smoking hash with one of the tourists. They hadn't said anything about the hash to keep him out of trouble with the police. But he was certainly fired. The photo from that day in Parque Central started to disintegrate in my pocket, eroded in its constant shift from my jacket to my raincoat, from my pack to my cloth shoulder bag. The corners had rounded and softened and the surface had lost its shine. It was gradually becoming the erasure of a photo. The picture of the dark-eyed guy was meeting a similar fate, even though I never took it out at all. It occurred to me that whatever happened to one photo might happen to the next, and whatever happened to one man might happen to the other, and then I couldn't get the idea out of my head. That's the cliff I jumped off. And so, just as I spoke to my mother, I started speaking to the two photos, too, asking them to take care, that sort of thing. I imagined that I'd fall in love with the stranger if I ever ran into him. He was Swedish, he was English, he was Norwegian. Good in bed. Reserved but reliable.

"He isn't lost, sweetie. Did it really take all these years of school for you to get so dim? He isn't *lost*," my mom would insist in the memory I invented as I talked with her in those days. She emphasized her syllables and shook her head. "He left because he wanted to. Do you think he would've snuck off like a thief if he really wanted to be with you?"

Those were the days of the impossible signs. *Neverest*. I saw the word everywhere, a distressing mantra. *N-Everest. Never-Est.* You're not going to find him. Don't stop to rest. Don't stop looking for him. Don't rest. You're not going to find him because he doesn't want you to. You lost him; he fell into a crack. Zero. Nothing. I'd dream about him plummeting to earth. I want to be left on the mountain, Bird. It's expensive to get a body down. I'd dream about his old wings; I'd see the scissors sink into the cloth. Back then. I'd wake in the middle of the night and look at the DVD. I don't mean I watched it: I'd take the disc in my hands and stare at it as if it could tell me something. Here, Bird, take my wings.

"That's a shitty present, Rafael," I'd reply. "A really shitty present."

Once I hurled it to the ground and it broke into three pieces. I threw up and cried. I put it back together with duct tape.

My mom spoke to me with completely opposite intentions from the ones that had brought me all the way to Kathmandu. Beyond the motive behind her advice, though, the advice itself was helpful. "You have to keep your antennae all the way up, sweetie. We get signs for a reason. You've gotten too many signs. The bum doesn't love you," she'd say.

"But I must have been given this wingsuit for a reason, Mom," I'd answer in my bedroom at the Luna Hotel, trying to untangle the cords and pack them up as best as I could. The only way to start a new chapter was to keep moving. *Never rest*. Julia has what it takes. "Never rest" won. No one wants to spend their lives telling themselves: if you'd just crossed the street you would have found him. Five minutes faster, and he would have been drinking coffee with you instead of exploding like a watermelon onto the ground. If you'd answered his email, he wouldn't have gone off to the peak where he froze to death.

I stopped waking up in the middle of the night, but what I started to call "nervous stomach" got worse. No matter what I ate or how much, I'd get indigestion. Sometimes I'd start to chew and almost immediately spit out the mouthful into a napkin or in the bathroom. This is going to make you sick. This is too greasy. You've eaten too much. There were many good reasons to get food out of my mouth. Technically it wasn't always vomiting; sometimes it was just the unwillingness to swallow. Your throat closes up. You gag and spit.

I took inventory at the Luna. Inward-outward. Two pairs of thermal underwear, three polar sweaters of varying thickness, one down jacket, one raincoat, three hats, wool gloves, polar gloves, and waterproof gloves. Sunglasses, sunscreen, a tinderbox, a flashlight, backup batteries, and my pipe. That was it. I stopped at the internet café before heading out. I ordered a beer and asked to use a computer. I was assigned the same one as always.

"Julia, we haven't heard from you in days. Please write us. Take care of yourself. Send us a note when you get this. Two lines. Just so we know you're all right. Let me know if you want me to start collecting your mom's things. Your aunt offered to do it. Hugs, blessings, sweet girl, we love you. Grigrí says meow."

I wrote three emails. This one:

"Dear Carlos, I'm writing from Kathmandu, I'm fine. Tell your kids and my cousins there's nothing to worry about. I'll write in a couple weeks, I'm leaving now. My stomach is fine. Tell me, what's the news on the house? Don't touch anything. I'll take care of it. Tell Grigrí that cats can't talk and if she doesn't want to shut herself away in that house you made for her then she shouldn't. Pet her for me. Let her out."

This one:

"Fabiiiii! I was inches away from finding him and then he disappeared again. I know he was fine a week ago. I'll write you when I'm back from the trekking trip. Ten days, maybe twelve. I'll send photos. My hotel is called the Luna. Love you. Give Lupe a hug for me and say hi to La Guairita. Do a traverse for me. Lots of landscape out here but only from a distance so far. No climbing. All searching."

And despite what Rafael repeated all the time—"Bird, what kind of freak spends two bucks to sit in front of a screen like a nerd? That's a whole meal, a spot for a sleeping bag at a hostel. A beer. Don't send me letters I can't touch. Forget it"—I wrote to him for the first time on the whole trip. Just because. What if he wasn't in Kathmandu anymore? I convinced myself. I assured myself that I'd only be able to reach him by email. "I can't stop dreaming about Everest, so that's where I'm going. Tomorrow I'll look for you. P.S. I have your wings."

The email was both brief and ridiculous. If it was very long, he was capable of not reading it at all. Or reading it backwards, the weirdo. If he read it, it was because he was in a village, not on Everest. And what would he do then—go back to Everest and look for me? It's not like that mass of rock and ice was some kind of corner bar, where people just show up and hang out. What's more, if he *was* on Everest or any other mountain, he wouldn't get my email for weeks. A useless email.

"Wait for me," I wrote him in a second email. Me and my unending ridiculousness. "I left my stuff at this hotel, Luna." And I copied down the contact information. Email me back or leave a note at the front desk. Underneath, in all caps: THERE'S FIFTY DOLLARS IN THE OUTER POCKET OF MY BEDROLL. TAKE THEM IF YOU NEED TO. DON'T WASTE IT ALL PARTYING. Then I typed out the details of the hotel again, and it'll sound strange, but I also added his own address and phone number in Caracas, in case he needed to go home and didn't know how. Finally, I wrote: Whatever you do, LET ME KNOW.

Before returning to the hotel, I stopped at KEEP to ask the girl at the store. She'd gotten her nose pierced and it was red as a tomato. I checked the messages on the bulletin board and found nothing. It looked like the colors were fading. I took a photo of the photos and the little Himalayan paper squares and took a self-portrait against them as a backdrop, becoming just another message, a note left for someone who wasn't there and wouldn't come back. I went out to the street and got lost. I bought a little bag of weed and filled my pipe. I slept.

I was in the airport by eight a.m. the next day. The top of my backpack contained a landscape slightly different than the one I'd started out with. The note that said *Wait 4 me*, creased now. The DVD coated in duct tape. The Roraima crystal hung on a leather string around the bear's neck. The plane had eight little windows on each side and two birds painted on the tail. It took forever for us to board and settle in. When we were finally ready and packed in like feathers in a down compression bag, the pilots got out. Bad weather. They went for a coffee. Passengers complained. Maybe Rafael didn't want to see me. Maybe there was some explanation for the setback and the wait on the tarmac. Sometimes the most important things are resolved in the most mysterious ways. Whatever happens, happens. If this thing isn't airborne in ten minutes I'll get off and forget all about it. Whatever happens, happens. Or maybe it'll take off and crash right then and there. It was as plausible for me to crash, as it was to find Rafael on the trekking trip, as seeing him suddenly appear in the doorway to the plane saying: Jesus, Bird, I finally found you. I've been looking for you everywhere.

I couldn't see much from the air. The tips of some astonishingly tall summits that look like ants next to Everest. When we flew over it, I thought—I knew—that this was the closest I'd ever be to the ceiling of the world. I didn't care. It's a gorgeous, formidable mountain I felt grateful I didn't want to climb and couldn't even if I did. It was there during the whole trip, deceptively close. Like a mother. People say the Lukla airport is the most dangerous in the world. The runway is incredibly short and you can't see it until it's underneath you. It's embedded into the mountains. When we landed, we were asked to hurry. There were passengers on the tarmac, and they looked exhausted, wrecked—waiting right there on the runway for their plane. And there were two little aircrafts still circling above us, waiting for us to move so they could land. From the bus, we saw the town market, the houses made of wood or stone, and then a tapestry of cultivated green hills. We stopped somewhere with no name. We started walking through a crush of people. Local residents, some carrying inhumane loads on their backs, yaks bearing even more weight, climbers on their way back. One limped past, a makeshift walking stick in hand. A sprained ankle, probably.

From that point on, I took out the photo to show people whenever I could. Leaving two prayer wheels behind, it occurred to me that I didn't know how to ask for what I was looking for. Buddhists surely don't ask, they must *utter* something, a secret code. I thought of Carlos. His book had nothing to say about incantations. In the end, I decided on this:

Please let Rafael appear. Please let Rafael appear. Please let him be okay. Please let him be intact. Please let it not feel horrible to see him. I remembered something Caboose would say: "Ask, because you never know what you're about to be given." Please, let everything be all right.

We came to a mound of sacred stones we were supposed to circle clockwise and we did. Five times. Everything has its own order there. It's not just about going; it's knowing how. He could be without a parachute, drunk in some village. I circled the stones again.

"Remember that bad news travels fast. By *jet*," Fabi says. "So does good news, but in chocolate bars," I always answer him.

I asked after him in two mountaineering cafés and three monasteries. I took lots of photos. I was riding a roller coaster. One day I'd feel optimistic: everything was going to turn out exactly as it was meant to, everything was going to be fine even if I didn't find him. At the end of the day, you're still in the Himalayas. The next day I'd find myself too weak to put one foot in front of the other. I was nauseated all the time. What's the point of being here, what good can it do me if I'm not going to summit and the guy I'm looking for has almost certainly forgotten me. Maybe he's dead. I don't even know why I'm looking for him. I don't know if I want him to be alive. Then the guilt. Little by little I got used to the cycles, and when I weakened again I'd try to focus on the landscape, or on the chimes of the bells strung around yaks' necks. An empty, hypnotic sound. A tunnel of sound in every clang that keeps vibrating until it vanishes into the next. Little things: the shades of green, my burning thighs, my lungs inflating, the clouds. The peaks around me, the bells again—I loved those bells. My photos, how many batteries I had left, what I still had to photograph. The pipe—where had I left it the last time, in which pocket of my pack, how would I fill it up at day's end so I could empty it once more before I went to sleep.

If he was alive, I thought, it was because I'd been carrying him around in my belongings. Safe if battered. The photos, the DVD, the letter, the bear, and the crystal couldn't just be abandoned. They were amulets, life insurances. On the bad days, I'd contemplate hurling them into the river or burning them, but I always ended up telling myself the same thing: I've got you. Don't worry, I've got you. They don't weigh anything anyway. Rafael's things, they're light, I'd tell myself. He could also be dead. In that case I couldn't rid myself of the only signs he'd left me on this planet. And they're light, I'd insist.

The ten days of overwhelming landscape and physical exhaustion, with their waves of pessimism and pinpoints of light, culminated in a collection of photos I mailed home along with the ones I'd taken at the beginning. The only thing I didn't want to lose. One afternoon I bathed in the river. I couldn't stand my dirty hair anymore, and I washed it too. It was a terrible faux pas (or was it on purpose?), and I ended up hypothermic, stuffed naked into my sleeping back, crying like a faucet. So much travel, so much verticality, so much tightrope-walking, just to kill myself with my own idiocy.

"You're going to freeze. Don't play games," said some of the other group members when they saw me getting into the water with my shampoo in one hand and my body rinse in the other.

"No worries, I never get cold," I lied. "I don't chill easily."

An hour later, bundled into the sleeping bag and shaking like an old washing machine, I wondered if I'd done it on purpose and why. "What game are you playing?" Then I thought about how I didn't want to die. That night I heard a tiger circling the campsite. Apparently it had eaten a calf somewhere nearby. I dreamed it was Rafael. Half-asleep at three in the morning, I decided to get out and look for him. When they found me, they told me I was so far gone in my altitude sickness that I was hallucinating. I can't explain it. Of course I knew that Rafael wasn't a tiger. The cure for altitude sickness is simple: you have to reduce your altitude. They made me. It was obvious to them. Between the frigid river-bath and the tiger-hunting expedition, I was clearly a danger to myself and to the success of the trip itself. Before making my way down, I started to vomit and no one believed me when I said it happened all the time. They thought I was in worse shape than I really was. "You have to go down. It's for your own safety," said Ram, before handing me off to the cook and one of his sherpas. Down we went. Otherwise, Neverest. I cried for the first two hours straight, but after that I didn't care about anything at all. I let myself drift in the sound of the bells. I stayed behind, hearing them move away and disappear and then intensify again as another trekking team approached. I photographed plants, hillside farms. The color of the earth, Nepalese children in their stacked-up clothing, their layers of cloth, one sweater on top of another, lots of red and black, embroidered garments, red cheeks, hair in braids or spiky as porcupines. Before we reached Kathmandu, I bought a bell. I wanted to take some small part of all that back with me when I went home. 🔔

Chapter XVIII

When you travel, you only know what you leave with. You don't know what you'll end up using, much less what you'll take home with you. Your luggage changes. Your gear gets lost or given away, exchanged. Stolen. Right around then, I gave away another Petzl headlamp and my Casio watch. Then I went straight to the usual corner to buy the usual stuff from the usual guy.

"Hello, madam!" he said happily. "I thought you went back to America!"

Dazed as I was, for the first time in ages I was glad to reencounter a map of my own. I stopped by the internet café. I sat at the keyboard with rubbed-off letters and drank a Lhasa beer, photographing it first. I'd received dozens of emails. Grigrí was fine. Carlos said hi and sent me blessings. My brother and sister were asking after me. Grigrí had figured out to get into her house. She missed her mama. My house was fine. Everything was in order and waiting for me. They hadn't moved so much as a single nail.

And that was it. Something from Fabi. Nothing important. A message from Lupe. They were back together. And Caboose had asked her to say: no moccasins, especially not without socks. Life is more beautiful without moccasins. Lupe said she'd set up an electrical system in those shoes. It shocks you if you stick your foot in. I left the café. I stopped by KEEP to check and photograph the bulletin board, where I found new signs of life. New colors, new stories. None spoke to me. I started to think about my trip home.

I discovered that the people at the store had become my friends; even the girl at the register greeted me with real affection. Her nose was better. Feeling comfortable, in good spirits, I went directly to Fire and Ice and ate a delicious four seasons pizza. I felt like just another resident of Kathmandu, and at the same time I wanted to go home. That night I lay in bed reading the world atlas from the front desk.

Downstairs the next morning, I was handed a recycled envelope with the address and previous recipients crossed out in pen, but it was well-sealed, and they told me it had spent five days in the hotel mailbox. They hadn't seen me arrive the night before, they hadn't expected me so soon, they apologized. I vaulted the stairs two at a time, my hands trembling. When I sat down on the bed, I already had the postcard from Meru Peak in my hands. *The Himalayas* was printed in cursive on the right-hand corner; beneath it, 6,600 mts. In his handwriting: *Bird, two and a half minutes in the air. It's not a jump. It's flying.* Below: Love, Rafael. I was absorbing it all, thinking about my next move, when I realized that the envelope also contained a slip of paper on the hotel letterhead: Little Bird, we're heading out for Meru Peak. It's time. 6,600 meters. I can't stop. Wait for me! And underneath it: I love you. I could stop a moving train. *Wait 4 me.*

Motherfucker. I checked my bed mat and the fifty dollars were gone. Son of a bitch. The parachute was missing from under the bed. I got into the shower in a cold sweat, and as soon as I felt the warm water spilling onto the skin of my belly I darted out and threw up. I soaped my body twice. I sat down on the ground and looked around me, opening my mouth, letting the water trickle in. I swallowed several mouthfuls and turned off the water, hard. I spit. *Si prega utilizzare solo acqua in bottiglia per bere o lavarsi i denti. N'utilisez que de l'eau traitée ou bouillie pour boire, pour vous brosser les dents. Verwenden Sie nur abgefülltes Wasser zum Trinken oder Zähneputzen. Please, use only bottled water for drinking or brushing teeth*, said a piece of paper taped beside the sink. As I came out of the shower, I lit the pipe to take away the taste.

I went to Smoke and found an abandoned newspaper and read an article about a trip to a liquid lake sunk over three kilometers deep into Antarctica, under the ice. A million years old. It said they were hoping to find new life forms—old ones, rather. That they'd make their way in with a three-kilometer hose, infiltrating a tunnel of hot water. Entering the lake meant entering the planet as it was a million years ago. At the end of the article, a sentence underlined in blue pen: The great mystery is what the waters of Ellsworth might hold.

Instead of food, I ordered a blue drink that tasted like syrup, a toast for Antarctica and for the new life that's actually the old. And for surprises. I ended up in the middle of a conversation about soccer.

"It was a handball," a Spaniard was saying.

"No way was it a handball, man," the other one answered, "because he touched it here, over here. That's not a handball, dude."

"That goal shouldn't have counted."

"It wasn't a handball. Give me a break."

"Fucking hell, Pasarella had the ball and then René jumped. It wasn't the most spectacular jump of all time, I'll give you that, but it wasn't a handball and he scored."

"I'm saying that goal shouldn't fucking count!"

I stood up, feeling that the floor was about to melt away under the force of a hose—filled with alcohol—and before I left I took a photo of the bar. It came out completely dark. I leaned against the doorframe. A psychological check-in to gather my strength. This tunnel isn't a wall. It's measured the other way around. It's going down.

One of the Spaniards came outside. With a Coke. He sat down on the sidewalk and held it out to me. He'd been in the Sahara and in Sri Lanka. When he started asking about my climbing partners,

I changed the subject as fast as a dyno. I gripped that hold. Foolproof.

"There's a little Hindu monkey who flew around carrying Sri Lanka on the palm of his hand. Have you seen it?"

"It's the symbol of courage," he answered. He told me its name, and that it's the Hindu representation par excellence of devotion and bravery. One of the most powerful deities. "And he's very famous in Sri Lanka. So? Where are you coming from?"

"I got hypothermia. I was on a trekking team at Everest base camp. It seems the down in my sleeping bag stopped warming up."

"Three drops of water and goodbye feathers and goodbye trip. It must've gotten wet."

"Maybe. It's weird. I have a bivouac sack."

"No way, lady. Bivouac sacks are too hot."

"It's a Kelty. Six hundred."

"The sack must have gotten soaked—with sweat."

"You have to be flexible about your plans. If you want to travel, you travel, and if you run into a climbing peak on the way, great, but if it gets too complicated, you leave it." I told him something like this. "I felt shitty, I was really cold, I felt like I was going to throw up, and I decided to come down."

"That's the best thing you could have done."

"Yeah."

"Don't obsess over it, though. If you think about it, on that *giro* you can't summit. That trip's just a tour. And it's fine. But there's nothing more inspiring"—he actually said *inspiring*, and I thought of Rafael and how he'd laugh at the showiness of this *gallego*—"than crowning a peak. Nothing more admirable than having a plan and carrying it out, or having a goal and fulfilling it. It's a demanding sport, but it's worth it," he said. How cheesy. I thought of Rafael.

"So where are your people, who did you come with?" he continued.

"I've gotten left behind, too. More than once, actually. I left Lupe once, in Roraima. She twisted her ankle and we left her there for a whole day and night. Anything could've happened to her. A snakebite, anything. It was fucked up. She stuck it out, poor thing. Not a word. Never complained. Awful. We were lucky. How about you? Have you been to La Gran Sabana?"

"Tell me, tell me more," he'd say once in a while, as if encouraging me to get comfortable so he could make his way up, or approach the midfield, so to speak.

"Roraima gets covered and uncovered by a blanket of clouds all day long. There's a sort of corridor along one side. The sky's blue and suddenly a cloud appears with a tail. Or, actually, the cloud is the tail, and the figure that follows is its owner. Lots of people have gone and tried to photograph it, but it hides from them. On the wall, it's just you and that cool air and the cushiony clouds. The rock and then white all around you. Beautiful. You can't see the planet down there. Buddy," I said abruptly, touching his back and giving him two little pats; who knows where I came up with such a bro-y gesture—"nice talking with you." I didn't know what time it was, but we must have been out there for quite a while, because the bar was empty and so was the street.

He came along without asking. Without asking, too, I continued my one-track monologue. "When there's just white, you're here all the time. Now. Here. You hear the voices of the rope team but you can't see anyone. The voices come from a different dimension." And meanwhile I was wondering how he'd say goodbye, if I wanted to let him into my room. If I wanted to refuse. It's amazing how many useless things you think. A story within another story. Two or three simultaneous voices. And you're in the middle, wondering which one you are. Which of the voices is yours. The Spaniard said goodbye at the door.

"Julia, dear, it's been a pleasure. Time to rest. Don't even think about tightrope-walking today. Sleep well," he said, and gave me a kiss on the forehead. I didn't know what I'd done to scare him off, but he practically sprinted away.

It was five in the morning when I called Fabi. I cried, had to leave him waiting on the line as I went to throw up and came back. I blew my nose on a shirt I tugged out of the top of my pack. It smelled like curry. I told him that Tibetans see a pilgrimage as the journey from ignorance to enlightenment, from selfishness toward connection with life.

"Where are you? Are you still in Kathmandu? Are you back?"

"Tell me, Fabi, how is it possible that he knows I'm here and just left me another fucking envelope? Goddammit, Fabi."

"Did you go to Everest? Did you see him?"

I didn't answer.

"Julia. Did you see Rafael? Do you know where he is? Did you see him?"

I told him.

"No way! That's insane!" He seemed to be laughing. "So you're telling me that he's on Meru? Holy shit. Son of a bitch!" He laughed more clearly now. "Did he take the wings?"

I hung up and lay down. When I woke up, I ran into the bathroom. It was after noon. I took a shower and went back to bed, feeling like my head was about to explode. Then I found a slip of paper under the door. Panicked, I unfolded it: I'll meet you for lunch. Outside your hotel at three. And beneath it: the Gallego. We started with the usual caution. The first time, you're not sure if you're going to like it, you don't know what the other person tastes like, smells like. He had a condom and put it on without my asking him to. I don't like it when men sweat so much, although Rafael does sweat a lot. The first time you don't know if the other's tongue will know where to look and how. There's just one way to find out. You have to undress, throw yourself into the descent, grip hard as you go downhill, close your eyes. Let it all roll around you.

Let the rhythm guide your movement. Let the movement go bright. Feel the breeze on your skin.

The last time I saw him was a continental breakfast where we exchanged email addresses and phone numbers. He was going back to Spain. I'd known that from the very beginning; he'd told me at the bar. Grateful, I photographed his face and hands, and I felt a strange sense of nostalgia, though I kept telling myself everything would be fine. Better, better all the time. I went out with him to the taxi, then returned to the table. I ordered a coffee with condensed milk. I photographed the jar of raspberry jam and what was left of the butter, because according to the Spaniard that morning, they tasted like me. No one had ever told me anything like that before, and I thought it was nice. Which was odd—I don't even like butter. ⊞

CHAPTER XIX

A tiny ad. A Fox canopy for sale: *Call for more info*. A phone number. Anyone could have written it. It wasn't his handwriting.

"How long has this ad been here?"

"I don't know. Three days? Since Thursday?" Her nose didn't look good; it was red and puffy around the piercing again.

"Has anyone asked about it? Did you see who put it there?"

"I haven't seen Rafael. Ram said he couldn't come back. Not within ten meters from the door, he said. He's not the one who left the paper," she finished confidently.

"Yeah, ten meters, I know."

"They called to leave the info. Ram wrote the ad."

I slipped the paper into the pocket of my raincoat and left without saying goodbye. The girl called after me, warning me not to even think about coming back to the store with him, yelling other things I couldn't hear. Her shrill voice followed me out the door. Rafael wouldn't leave his wings behind. I'd rather die than travel wingless, Bird. My knees were shaking. I went in search of a rickshaw. I tried to get into the first one that stopped, but then I had to let it go and run toward a corner to vomit. People parted around me. It was hot. Heavy air. Rain was coming. Three dogs materialized and started licking at the bitter puddle on the ground. I moved away as quickly as I could, startled and repulsed and wanting to forget the whole scene, and made my way to a stand selling coconut water. I took three sips and tossed it into the trash as another rickshaw approached. There was a lot of dust, too much heat.

It took me forever to reach the building. Four floors and a roof-top terrace, faded curtains of different colors, two windows covered with batik blankets. The doorbells, seven of them, looked like light switches. Their cables coated the façade and entered each room through the windows. I rang every single buzzer, but no one leaned out. I pushed at the front door. It was open. A dark hallway and some narrow concrete stairs. I went up to apartment 31 and heard footsteps when I banged on the metal door.

It opens a crack. An eye peering through. The door shuts. No one opens it, but I know that no one's moving, either: the person is still there. I think I can hear him breathing. My heart beats fiercely. I knock again, though what I really want is to shoot back down the stairs. I think of the rickshaw man who's waiting out front. If he doesn't open the door by the time I count to five, I'm leaving. One.

Two.

Three. I lean out the window toward the street. Kids playing soccer. No. I look again. The rickshaw's gone. Shit. That's what you get for shelling out upfront. You don't pay a taxi driver if you want him to wait.

Four.

Five. I walk toward the stairs, almost on tiptoe, trying to stretch out the five, letting the person who doesn't want to open the door not open it. What's not meant to be won't happen. On five, I'll go. If I count to five, I'll go, I say, but just as I start to leave, I hear the door behind me. I have my back to it, I'm leaving, I'm gone—but I turn.

Very skinny. Short, short hair. A new gaze in a familiar body I didn't greet. All the skin of my back standing on end. To stay or to go. My amygdala struggling. Berkeley. Red Rocks. Now that you're here, stay. Since you didn't leave, fuck it all.

"Are you just going to stand there?"

Inside, a mostly empty room, no gear in sight. Beer cans. Not so much as a dirty dish in the sink. The rest of the kitchen, spotless. To run or to embrace. A sleeping mat and sleeping bag on the floor. The wings in a corner, wrapped up and packed. BASE jump or tightrope. To flee or keep going. He came closer. He gripped my shoulders. He didn't hug me.

"Why are you here?" He let go, avoiding my eyes. "What do you want?"

"A glass of water."

I watched him move away, wiping his hands on his pants. He had a tattoo on the nape of his neck. An eagle, wings outstretched, that also looked like a dragon. He filled a glass from the faucet. *Verwenden Sie nur abgefülltes Wasser zum Trinken oder Zähneputzen.* I thought he was opening a drawer. I felt my knees falter. He walked toward me, held out the glass. I took two long sips and then bolted toward the bathroom, knelt in front of the toilet. *Si prega utilizzare solo acqua in bottiglia per bere o lavarsi i denti.*

"Do you need anything? Fuck. You still haven't gotten over your pukefests after all this time?"

"I'm fine. Maybe a beer?"

"What did you come for, Bird?" he asked, motionless, his arms crossed over his chest, his torso tilted slightly away from me.

"A beer."

He turned and moved toward the fridge. "I come all the way to the ass-crack of the world for some peace and quiet and then I find out you're hanging out down the street. How's your mom?"

I shook my head, staring at the floor. "What?"

"Oh, shit." He stood up and rubbed his hands on his pants again. "Do you want another beer? I meant the house, your things. School. How's everything?"

"Still working on this one, thanks," I said, gesturing with the bottle. "Everything's all set. Graduated. All set."

"Good, good, Bird," he answered, like when you summit and descend as fast as possible. You celebrate later. Or you don't. You don't celebrate. "You have to see the photos," he continued, lobbing the can into the trash from a distance and approaching the fridge again. "It's a small apartment, but the trash can's far away. You gotta save energy," he joked. "Incredible jump, Bird. The most impressive thing I've ever seen. You have to see the photos," he insisted, backlit by the refrigerator.

Like returning from a trip to discover that not a single piece of furniture is where you left it. Like walking into someone else's house and discovering your own furniture inside. Like opening the drawers of the house I've always lived in and finding them empty.

"I don't know why I came. Don't call me Bird anymore. What's the deal with that tattoo?"

"You're shitting me," he said, stepping toward me with his brows furrowed, eyes myopic. "You're saying that you came to Kathmandu and you've spent a month wandering in circles and breathing down my neck and now you show up on my doorstep to say you don't know why? You're seriously driving me crazy. And now I can't call you Bird. Whatever you say. *Fuck*, girl. Whatever you fucking say."

He sat down on the floor with his head on his hands. I drew closer.

"I was worried. And I didn't know where to go."

"Its name is Garuda. It's an eagle," he said, lifting his face.

To hold. To kiss. His three moles. The new tattoo. He grasped me by the legs and I sank to my knees. We ended up on the floor. He opened my legs, shoved me toward the ground, pushing into my shoulders. He yanked down my pants. The film started rolling and I pulled off my sweater and hurried with his shirt. I was drenched by the time he was inside me. His lean buttocks in my hands, digging my fingers into him, his powerful thighs. I felt the bones of my spine striking the floor to a wild, violent beat. Quickened waves. Percussive swells. No pain, no pain. Precipice. He lifted me up, grabbed my iliac crests like climbing holds to push deeper into me. I yelled. At the end I bit his shoulder just in time, just hard enough for him to pull away, to keep his semen from spilling into me. He came outside, onto himself, and he hugged me. I felt the sweat pooling together with the thick liquid between us, his breath on my neck. He turned me around and stretched out onto my body. Compressed there, I thought of the red rocks in the park with the same name. I felt sweaty, suffocated by the dead weight I didn't want to carry, something crushing me into the ground. I gave him a firm, gentle push to one side and ended up on my back. Relief. There was a crack on the ceiling. I stared at it and my eyes filled. I dried them quickly. I sat up and put on my shirt and pants.

"Ready? Already?" he said, pulling me lightly toward him.

"I'm thinking of Goa. I want to go to the beach. I need water. Sea breeze."

"Cats don't like the ocean. You know that." He flicked a tongue along my arm. Licked me again. "Clean off like this."

I wiped off the cold saliva with my palms. I went to the bathroom, turned on the faucet, stripped down. He appeared with my underwear in hand.

"You had me worried. You came into the apartment with that look on your face, and I thought, Ohhh man, here comes the drama. Shit. Then you throw up, you say you're leaving, we fuck, you run off to the bathroom, and now you decide you're leaving again and I can't contact you anymore. So? I don't know about you, but now that you're here, I want more." And he grabbed me by the arm, pulling me close.

"Could you give me a second to take a shower?" I said, looking at the eagle. It was pretty big, impossible to ignore. I hoped he'd take off and leave me alone, though I didn't dare ask.

He sat on the toilet lid and started rolling a joint.

"A gorgeous flight, Julia. I thought of you so much. You'd love it. I thought of you so much. Three days to base and then five more all the way up. That's when I got sick. I was puking my guts out, like you, but worse. Want some?" He passed me the joint as I dried myself off with a bit of shammy cloth. "I thought I'd abort the whole mission. But no, they gave me a pill. We have to find out what it's called. Maybe it'll help you. And after that it was all gravy."

People say you hear better if you close your eyes, but sometimes it's the other way around. I left him in the bathroom and sat with the joint on the living room floor. I'm lying down in the grass. I feel the dampness under my skin, and the part of my clothing that touches the earth is a little colder. I wonder if it's rained. I hear a voice in the distance, the wind striking the wings, the white landscape. "...So cold, Bird. Seriously, I always think of you. We have to keep going together, now that you've come all the way here...there's so much I have to show you." My eyes are closed, my weight pressing into the ground. My throat stings, my chest burns. *Numb is good.* Many lives ago, you invited me to fly with you. Eyes closed. Stretched out on the grass, I feel the wetness under my skin, the cold earth below me. I wonder if it's rained and where the moisture comes from. Eyes closed, weight pressing into the ground. It's expensive to get a body down from the mountain, you said once. *Numb is good.* I want to be left wherever I'm found, you said.

"You're going to like it when you grow up," he said, as I returned what was left of the joint. "Want to go? A *dahl* from the corner?" He grabbed his keys, walked toward the door. I had my raincoat and my backpack on. "Leave them here. My treat. And it's not going to rain." When I didn't answer: "You win. Don't be mad. I'm exhausted, to be honest. A nap's not a bad idea. You're the boss, okay. You say Goa, Goa it is."

"I mean it. It's over."

"You're right. Life can't be all work and no play," he laughed.

I took three photos from the doorway. Rafael appears in the last one, bowing. I left him the two ruined photos, his and the appropriated one, and the duct-taped DVD. I handed him the crystal, but he returned it to me and I let him. I took the stairs down three at a time. I stretched up an arm to take a photo of myself. The cables scratching the façade of the building. The window no one had peered out of.

The rickshaw was still there. ◫

Chapter XX

I boarded the train. The wheels started to turn and screech, and the landscape blurred with particles rising up from the ground. I had an assigned seat, but it was the usual deal when I stepped into the train car: the tickets are only good for boarding, and once you're on, it's survival of the fastest. I sat on top of my pack in a corner of the aisle. It turned out to be a slow local train making constant stops, which meant I'd be able to sit in a seat with a back within a couple hours. I fell asleep.

I jolted awake. It seemed that a man had run through the car, tripping and clawing his way through the few passengers left in the middle of the aisle, and as I opened my eyes they were shouting and cursing at the shadow of the ghost, now gone. Then the conductor made his way past, saying something into his radio, and two men who were also yelling, gesturing to the outside, swiping at each other. I peered through the minimal open space to get a glimpse of the window, and in the distance I could see the man running along a yellow plain.

When I arrived, pushed and pulled and jammed into the funnel of people trying to exit the station, I ended up next to a pair of backpackers, a couple. I was intrigued by his clothes. His name was Dylan and he was wearing an apple-green and gold sari over khakis and a t-shirt. Sandals, too. Her name was Federica. We bumped into each other in the chaos and laughed, and as we made our way to the other side I took advantage of our brief complicity to ask them a couple questions. I had hours to go before my bus; I needed to eat and change money. They invited me to have lunch with them nearby and talked as we went. They'd been traveling and living between India and Pakistan for a year and a half. Almost two, Dylan corrected.

"It's my form of protest," he said, signaling to his clothes when he noticed my curiosity. "We're trying to raise awareness about the problem of violence against girls and women in these two brother countries."

"We work with an organization," Federica explained, visibly embarrassed, in an attempt to excuse Dylan's patronizing tone. "Naarayani. India and Pakistan may be brothers, but they live in conflict. The same could be said of any group, any couple. We're all brothers and sisters, aren't we? But closeness causes friction. Violence against women is one of their shared problems. The rope always snaps where it's most fragile."

They looked at my camera, asked what I did. They wanted to know how long I'd be staying, about my plans in India. They invited me to join them.

"There's not much money. We're looking for someone to document our activities. We work with recycled goods. We make these handbags," said Federica, showing me the one she had slung over her shoulder. "Look, this is where it opens. We give talks, hand out information. From how to use contraceptives to how to file a complaint and find work. How to open a bank account."

"That's when you learn they don't even have any papers," said Dylan, lifting one side of his sari, a gesture I soon saw was reflexive. "If you're going to teach them how to open a bank account, first you have to go with them to get their papers. No one helps them. They don't even dare set foot in the bank. That's how they're most useful to society. Ignorant, scared, undocumented."

"It's a big project. Five locations: Bangalore, Delhi, Islamabad, and Karachi."

"Not that big," Dylan answered with a smile I found condescending. "There are actually just a few of us. Two or three souls per city." Without my realizing how, we'd arrived, and we were taking off our shoes. You were supposed to wash your hands in a copper bowl as you went in. The Indian background music was unbearable. You had to shout to talk. To my amazement, the place was full. It had a fixed lunch menu.

"It sounds so interesting," I told them. You say "interesting" when you don't know what to say, or when you feel like running in the opposite direction.

"Just think—a woman photographer? Incredible! You'll win their trust right away," said Fede, making her way toward one of the tables. She greeted the hostess by bringing her palms together at her forehead and bowing slightly. I tried to imitate her, but I couldn't. I smiled and took a seat.

"It's just that my mom died a few months ago. It's a long story. I have to clean out her things, sell my house. I have a cat. I have to go home. Her name is Grigri."

"Forget being sad and go to Bangalore."

"No...I mean, I'm not sad anymore."

"That's where we have our headquarters, and where my master lives. Who takes care of your cat?"

"You have no idea how hard it is for me to get her out of Bangalore," Dylan joked as he made room on the table for the three *thali* platters, which I correctly guessed would be vegetarian.

"It's the only place where we have an office," Fede explained, dipping her *chapati* in a dish of *palak paneer*.

187

"...and where Lakshmi lives. First, acid in the face at twelve years old. Her stepfather. Then her uncle. If she was poor before, imagine her now. Marriage? No one wants her."

"She's our assistant. Listen: you go. You visit the Center. You visit the school. You'll love it, I promise. And you'll meet my master. He's unbelievable. God. Being in a country where a *zampetta* is as natural as in Italy—priceless," she said licking her fingers after swallowing another mouthful of spinach-dipped bread.

Dylan nodded and did the same. "We can't pay you, but you'd get room and board. And if Masterji knows you work with us, he won't charge you," he continued.

"But I don't do yoga. I want to see Goa, go to the beach. I just want to rest. I've heard it's beautiful there."

"Try it. You'll like it, I swear. I can call, if you want, and you can go straight there. There's a *batik* class in the next few days and then a march where we're going to give out the dyed shirts. You could take the photos."

"I don't have any more money or any more time," I said, pushing at the metal tray.

"You won't regret it. Everything happens for a reason. Just think— the three of us met in that ocean of people. And it turns out you have a camera, you speak English, and you don't have anyone else."

"You talk just like Tomás," I said, smiling, "a friend who says everything's causal. Not *casual*, a coincidence—causal. But everyone travels like this! Everyone travels like everyone else, with a camera. And almost all of them speak English."

We laughed and I thought the subject was closed.

"Leave Goa for the end of your trip. Actually, don't go to Goa at all," Fede resumed minutes later, when we were leaving the restaurant. "It's a tourist trap. Work with us, *dai*. I can call if you want," she persisted. "They'll have a taxi meet you at the bus station. It's really fun to see your name on the sign, to have someone waiting for you instead of struggling to make your own way." Apologizing then, she added, "It's not that it's on your way, but it's in the south. And you're going south."

I showed her my ticket. "Here, look. I already booked a ticket to Goa. Everything. Everything's all set."

"A Deluxe bus? No!" she exclaimed, inspecting the ticket. She looked at Dylan. "Darling, look at this! *Giulia* bought a Deluxe ticket!"

"It was the same price! It's not like I spent a fortune," I said, ashamed. I must look so contemptible to them, I thought, traveling on the Deluxe line.

"Of course! What did I tell you?" she said to Dylan. "*Poverina!*"

Poor thing? But it's a Deluxe! I wanted to tell her. That's when I learned this company runs only night buses, and that their routes were notorious for gropings, thefts, and other abuses. I'd chosen a window seat so I could look out at the landscape, which made everything worse. *Landscape?* On a night bus? I could almost hear my mother saying. The thing is, I started to grasp what should have been obvious: the ticket that gets you traveling through India in the dark, as a woman, trapped in a corner, is a thoroughly un-privileged ticket into a total nightmare. The golden rule: don't book a window seat unless you're traveling with someone else. I know this now.

"The thing is that it's hard to get anyone to defend you," Dylan said, trying to quiet Fede. "Men cover for each other here. They laugh at tourists. They play deaf. But if anything happens, Julia, if you yell really loud, I'm sure the driver will stop."

"I guess there's nothing I can do about it, though. There were no seats left on the train," I responded, discovering that I was resigned to it. Deep down, I didn't really care. You don't travel so far for such a minor scare. I didn't say anything else.

"It's because it's Holi. Everybody goes to the beach."

That's when I noticed how people were looking at us. Staring at Dylan's attire, girls covered their mouths with their hands, hid behind each other, laughed uncontrollably. Two men bumped into him on purpose, hard.

"You have to stop doing this. It's going to happen to you again. Please stop doing this, even if it's just for me," Federica said to him, quickening her step and grabbing him by the arm.

"I'm not scared!" Dylan retorted as he adjusted the sari over his shoulders. "I wear it and I'm proud. Someone has to do it."

"I know! I know you're not scared. But I don't want to end up in the hospital again. Do you have a towel?" she continued, still walking hurriedly but turning to look at me now. "Because there aren't any at the house. They give you sheets but not a towel." She turned to Dylan. "We can give her one, right? Or the sari!" She laughed. "Give her the sari and our problems are solved. At least you're traveling light," she said to me. "You're not weighed down. Later everything gets to be a burden. In any case, if it's a beach you want, don't go to Goa. It's a tourist trap. Palolem is cheaper, there's organic food, two yoga schools. One's called Shiva Shakti. That's the best one, and the vibes are great. When you get to Bangalore, go here," she added, handing me a piece of paper with the address.

Shit! Federica had it all planned out. A man suddenly cut in front of us. I jumped. So did Fede and Dylan.

"Hash?" The man gestured with his hand and expression in a way that indicated the way we were supposed to go.

"Is your camera good?" Fede asked. We walked through a narrow doorway that opened out onto a kind of café.

A large woman was sitting at a table in the corner. She didn't bat an eye. Curled up on the ground a little closer to us was a rangy dog who pricked up its ears as we came in, then lowered its head to rest on its crossed front paws. There was a Coca-Cola ad in Hindi taped up on the chipped green wall. We took a seat on a mat.

I'm not sure how much time passed. As we smoked, I entertained myself reading some TV gossip and Bollywood celebrity magazines that were all but falling apart. The man left the three of us there and slipped outside again. I took photos of the place, the magazines, and Federica, who embarked on a traditional Indian dance performance, arranging her hands into *mudras*, shifting her eyes from side to side like a lizard. We were overcome with fits of laughter. I hadn't laughed in a long time. My abs hurt by the end. As we left, they invited me to come meet a friend of theirs from the NGO. I still had hours to kill before I left, and strangely enough I didn't want to be alone. So I didn't refuse. 卍

Chapter XXI

By eight p.m., when the bus was scheduled to leave for Goa, Fede and I were old friends. She didn't say another word about yoga or Bangalore or women or violence. She talked instead about the Goa scene and gave me a couple of names and addresses. Before boarding the bus, I turned to say goodbye. I blew her a kiss and she called after me, jumping up and down like a little girl, pointing to a bus next to mine: "Palolem is better! Go to Palolem!"

There I was, under a thatched ceiling, staring out at the sea like a star. The town had two main dirt roads, a juice store, and various bars and cafés. A street market selling supposedly very Indian clothes and accessories, made just for tourists: metal deities, honey and sandalwood incense, handbags and cloths stamped with the images of Lakshmi, Hanuman, and Ganesh. A fruit market, several air-conditioned internet cafés, and a tourist agency that opened at six in the evening. Tourists passing through, local residents trying their damndest to look like tourists, and tourists who seem to have always been there and will be there forever. People who came for a break and haven't left in ten years.

Anyone who's been to Choroní knows what I'm talking about. Take that up about four notches. If Choroní's a six, Palolem's a ten. If you've never been to either, imagine a beach that's essentially a nightclub in the daytime—a twenty-four-hour club, better put—and a town at the same time. A village both traditional and hipster. An exotic place, with good waves, half-naked people walking around everywhere, happy and free at least in appearance, that smells of weed and incense anywhere you go. That's what it's like.

When I arrived, I walked toward the coast while making careful note of key spots. Fede's bar and vegetarian restaurant, Shiva Shakti, the internet café. Rob's corner. The most important thing is to track down the key spots, Bird. The rest happens all by itself. Rafael calls them the necessaries. After so many years, the people you've loved or love don't disappear so easily. They stay with you like a coating on your skin. Like a scar on a cerebral convolution.

People in Goa looked comfortable, overheated but calm, relaxed. Too many tattoos, some newly minted: arms smeared with sunblock later revealed new Hanumans, new OMs, fresh letters in Sanskrit. When we'd go to the beach, my mom would grease us up with Nivea cream; it came in a spherical screw-top can, royal blue. She'd daub our noses and cheeks and shoulders with a thick, cold coat. Armor against the sun. I hadn't been there more than five minutes or walked more than four blocks from the bus station when I'd run into five discount tattoo stalls. Three small tattoos for the price of two, or two medium-sized ones for the price of one. After just a few hours on a bus, and after so many weeks of sheathing my arms in long-sleeved shirts, of covering my head with shawls regardless of mood or weather, I was suddenly surrounded by wandering abs and love handles, by shamelessly bare torsos. I started stripping down, too, in the middle of the street, as I got closer and closer to the sand and felt that my sandals and then my feet were digging deeper and deeper in. It was incredibly hot, but the ocean was just a few steps away. I turned left and saw the stilt huts maybe five hundred meters in the distance.

One, two, three, from left to right. I climbed the stairs of the one I guessed was mine. It was a little run-down; one of its thatched walls was damp and looked on the verge of collapse. It was the only one available, though, so I didn't complain. In fact, I ended up sharing it with someone else for a few hours. The girl was leaving and didn't mind my settling in right away—that's what I was told at the front desk. I had no objections. I didn't care. I called out a greeting as I walked in, but there was no response. I sat at the edge of the only bed there was, then lay down.

Matter is energy, Energy is Light, We are all light beings, Albert Einstein, said a piece of paper taped to one of the thatched walls. I fell asleep. The ocean always makes me sleepy. I was jolted awake by a woman's voice.

"Hari OM!"

A hardy girl, her skin leathery from the sun, wrapped in two sarongs just like the ones I'd seen in the market, but faded. She smiled at me and joined her palms at her forehead in a slight bow. I quickly learned that my fleeting friend was learning to read auras.

"I can see plant auras, cow auras, dog auras. Human auras only sometimes. It's harder with people," she said in a confidential tone. We went out to walk on the beach. She stopped a couple of times and stood stock-still in some sort of exercise. "The Master says you have to practice with everything, with any living thing. The point is to practice without caring about the results: 'Practice, practice, and all is coming.' That's what he says."

I stood and watched her, feeling the sun simmer on my skull and my feet scorch, not saying a word—who was I to interrupt her in her summit-moment? If you can even have a summit-moment when you read an aura. Who knows what it's like. Both times, I was lucky; she started walking again before my feet turned into jellyfish.

"You can't rush it. Like I said, it's harder with people. Bright, clear yellow around the head means intelligence, wisdom, and success. If the brightness, tone, or location change, the meaning changes, too. Bright yellow around the chest can mean compassion, patience, and desire for surrender. So you have to look close-ly. You could get it wrong and screw up someone's life if you tell them something that's not true. That," she insisted, "is why it's so important to practice."

We each bought a coconut from a little stall and continued along the sand. "Have you ever eaten coconut from a coconut?"

"What?"

"It has flesh inside—have you seen it?" Erika asked, unable to hide her own astonishment. It was then that I realized how young she was.

"How long have you been traveling?"

"It's not the amount of time that matters, it's how the journey changes you," she answered, furrowing her brow a bit and staring out into the horizon. "When we head back, we'll ask the guy to split them open. You'll see. He'll open them up right in front of us. Any-way. If someone passes close by, they can take your energy away. I don't mean *you*"—she touched me gently on the arm—"your vibes are good. You're light. But it's best to watch out. Someone else can interrupt your flow just by touching you. That's how people get sick," she concluded, scraping at little bits of coconut meat with the straw she'd used to drink the water.

My aura was light blue, very light. "Don't treat the spiritual realm like it's a game," she said. A pink trace suggested a depar-ture. "Have you said goodbye to anyone lately?"

"I'm not treating it any way at all. I don't take it lightly or seri-ously. I'm not a believer." I stopped, bit my tongue, softened my voice: "It's just that I came to the beach to relax. I'm taking a break."

I told her I was a climber, that I'd just had an experience of be-ing very cold, that I needed to unwind. "I brought supplies to teach tightrope classes. Do you think people would be interested in learn-ing how to slackline?" I improvised.

She smiled and placed a hand on my shoulder. "You'll see. Lots of people start out like that here." Like what? I thought. Lying, fleeing, telling half-truths? "But sooner or later, everyone gets it. There's a reason why you're in India, you'll see. No one comes here by accident. It's all karma. I have an extra yoga mat. It hasn't been used much and it doesn't smell bad. I can leave it for you if you want. But tell me, how is it that you came to the south?"

"If I told you, you'd miss your bus."

"It doesn't leave for six more hours!"

"Exactly."

We both knew I wasn't going to tell her anything. Better to emerge unscathed. To avoid the subject, I told her to drop it and stop reading my aura, or least to not tell me what she saw if she saw anything. "Unless you see a dead body somewhere around here," I said, trying to laugh. We both fell silent.

"It's a shame."

"What?"

"It's a shame. Because I like you. It would've been nice to have you as a guest," she said. We were on our way back now, and the man was splitting open the two coconuts with a machete. The coconut was as tender as Jell-O inside. "I'd stay with you another couple days. But I can't. I'm going with my master to Osho's house. They invited him, and he chose me as his companion. We're leaving today and we'll be back in two weeks. I can't not go."

You can tell. You can always tell. She clearly recognized that there was something suspicious about her story; it was as if she had to excuse herself. "My master is so generous. It's such an opportunity, such an experience. Going to Osho's is usually very expensive, but since he's taking me with him, I won't have to pay." Finally, she added, "I'm sorry to leave you by yourself. I know you just got here. But—can you imagine? Going to Osho's ashram?"

I could. I imagined—remembered, really—what I'd heard about his orgies and philosophy of free love, the accusations of sexual abuse, the dress code. Everyone had to wear the same color, depending on the time, or the day. When they were dressed at all, that is: there were nudist parties, too. She didn't mention any of that. Actually, she did, but just the colors. Wide-eyed, she explained that Osho had three houses in India; that between your arrival and your departure you have to dress in white or burgundy depending on the activity you're taking part in; that there's scheduled sitting meditation, walking meditation, and dancing meditation; that you do karma yoga in the kitchen and by cleaning the house or washing the others' clothes. And that the best part is the dances.

"You've really never heard about Osho?'

"Nothing."

"You're not allowed to dance with your eyes open and if you bump into someone you have to touch them. If you like what you feel, you stay there, and if you don't you keep going. All with your eyes closed."

She told me that the ashram had black marble floors and walls and that one of the three temples is a pyramid.

"That's where you let everything go. You're cleansed and purified and you come out seeing the world in a different light. Those dances cleanse you of your history, you know. I'd take you with me if I could."

When we were back at the hut, she gathered up her things to make room for mine in the closet, as she called it. The closet consisted of two bamboo shelves. All of her belongings must have amounted to five sets of clothing, a couple of books, and two sandalwood carvings. She left me some Sai Baba incense.

"Leave the front light on after dark. And use the padlock even if you're just going to the bathroom. Careful with invitations, careful with people who offer you weed, because sometimes it's laced. Flow, be light, this is a magical place. But don't forget—you're alone here. You're alone."

I wondered what the next novelty would be. Palolem, Kathmandu, Sierra Nevada del Cocuy. She carried on this way, giving me instructions I stopped hearing, although I stayed put, watching her collect her things. How complicated could it be to stuff three shirts into a little pack?

"There are lots of thieves at night. They open the door and take everything. They turn the rooms upside-down and leave them totally empty. Anyway, I paid for the month—it's cheaper that way, the hut, renting it by the month. So don't let them charge you for the four days left. The manager's a cheat." She ducked under the bed to pull out her yoga props. "Mind like a sieve! I almost forgot these. Can you imagine?" she laughed. Two wooden blocks, a blanket, and several tangled-up ropes. I thought they looked like instruments of torture. I've always been puzzled by yogis' ropes and sandbags, how people tie themselves up and climb into looms to stretch out properly, attain liberation, all that stuff.

"How much do I owe you?"

"Nothing! Here, take this," and she tossed me her mat, which opened as it fell. The ends were corroded and looked somewhat stained or dirty. Where the feet would go, I guessed.

"You don't carry much," I told her, laughing, when I looked at the empty room around me and at her pack, tiny and loose-fitting despite how badly she'd stored, removed, and re-accommodated everything. That's what we share at the end of a trip: a light load. The possibility of assembling and disassembling a home in five minutes. The ability to carry it on your back. The chance to start over wherever you are.

"If you're still here in two weeks, give or take, we'll see what we can do," my friend said, smiling. She closed her pack and lifted it to her shoulders. "When I'm back. Whether you stay or go. Whatever you want. If I even come back"—she smiled again and almost winked—"because you never know."

"Listen. There are lots of ways to call in a favor," I told her without thinking. Erika had undergone a sort of regression over the past few hours. She looked younger and younger, less and less experienced. "Sometimes you think you get to go places for free, Erika, but you don't. Nothing is free," I continued. Now that I'd unbitten my tongue, I thought, why hold back. There I was, lecturing at the podium. "Remember. You're going to be alone there. There, just like here, if you're alone, you're alone." And I smiled.

I suddenly thought about this trip, how I'd been meeting people only once and never seen them again. There are only secondary characters in this story, I thought. In the end she left me the yoga mat—there was no escaping that part, but at least she didn't ask me any more questions. She walked toward the door but turned to look at me before walking through it, brought her palms together at her chest, and bowed in a way she made look completely natural.

"*Namaste.*"

I lowered my head a little, trying to acknowledge her gesture, and smiled. Then I bid her goodbye with my instinctive Western greeting, feeling clumsy, orphaned, waving a hand from side to side. I took a photo of her, the green pack on her shoulders, against the sea.

Pointing to a corner near the bed, she added, "Oh, and it gets wet there when it rains. I lay out a towel and then dry it in the sun."

Hari OM and her left hand forming the peace sign, or V for Victory, or the summit sign, was the last thing I heard and saw before she vanished behind the leafy door. She looked happy.

I found myself in bed again, suspended there like a star, looking up at the thatched roof. The hut was nearly empty. Just an image of Hanuman—he'd followed me all the way here—on a wall, the taped-up Einstein quote, a purple yoga mat—mine now, I guessed—and a yellow sarong printed with tiny OM symbols, rolled up in a corner. I photographed each object and then my objects on the bed. An inventory. Ram had ended up with almost all my high-mountain and travel gear after the Neverest incident. So I only had two pairs of pants, three t-shirts, my flip-flops, and my bathing suit. I was left with my music, my passport, a crumpled plane ticket, the crystal from Roraima, the bear, some rupees, some dollars. And the yak bell.

I've never forgotten Clementina, the turtle from a story I read as a little girl, who carries on her shell a load of objects she was given by her he-turtle. Gifts she hasn't asked for and doesn't want, gifts that come to be an unbearably heavy burden. One day she can't take it anymore. Tired of the parcel she's become, she leaves the whole useless heap on the edge of a lake. She goes off alone, leaving behind the he-turtle, her shell, and the impossible weight, swimming freely through the water. She never comes back.

In the hut, then, I thought that would be all. When I went back to Caracas, I'd have no souvenirs from the trip, nothing, not a single piece of cloth, not a single pashmina shawl. After the scores I saw in Kathmandu. Nothing. Just the bell. I thought of it, turned onto my side, and pulled it out of the top of my pack. There I was, playing with it, shifting around in the bed and staring into space, thinking and looking at myself ironically when the thought came: my austerity was my discipline. There I was, under the palm-frond ceiling, looking out at the ocean like a star. That was all. 卐

Chapter XXII

I noticed the commotion around lunchtime. I thought it was strange that no one had told me anything about it, and that I hadn't noticed it myself when I arrived. The town was going crazy. A solar eclipse was on its way, and everyone—the tourists who looked like tourists and the locals who looked like tourists and the tourists who looked like locals, and me, too, soon enough—was looking for negatives or X-rays to use as filters. Some market stalls were selling them for a hundred rupees. I didn't believe in temporary blindness, but better safe than sorry. I bought a jet-black negative.

I walked along the other dirt avenue toward the vegetarian place and ordered a lentil burger. It was glorious. Who knows if it was the burger itself or the pound of Heinz ketchup. On my way back, I was handed two flyers advertising a "midnight beach party." On the sand, five guys in black shirts and jeans were assembling a platform and transferring cables this way and that. Crazy heat. Above the platform, surrounded by flower wreaths, was a sign that said Om Shanti.

I walked toward the hut. I climbed the stairs, went in, changed my clothes. I was coming back down in my bathing suit—which I found old, worn-out, frumpy, with the Lycra strained and the colors faded—when I ran into a guy walking up the staircase of the hut next door. It was very, very hot.

When got to the top, my neighbor greeted me with the peace sign. Twice in one day seemed excessive. I guess I'll have to get used to it, I thought. He was wearing a huge pair of sunglasses. Bug eyes. He was skinny and very pale and wore a heavy gold chain around his neck. His back was bony and lightly curved. A vampire, Lupe would call him. There's something about India. I don't know; people reveal themselves. It must be the illusion of distance. Today, nothing's far away. A summit's far away, a cliff. The bottom of the ocean and the Antarctic lakes. A country is always close by. I wrapped myself with the sarong I'd brought as a towel; its value suddenly appreciated. How can Lycra stretch out like that?

We said hello and chatted about the eclipse. He offered me a negative he was holding in his hand.

"I've got one," I said, showing it to him.

The skinny guy had a strange accent. Sitting on the steps of his hut, he offered me a cigarette, which I accepted. He told me his itinerary. He'd just graduated. He talked about his impressions of the trip, the trance parties in Goa. Apparently they had nothing on the ones in Beirut. He talked about the Indians.

"They're all a bunch of thieves, always trying to figure out how to rob you. They're dumb and they touch you all the time. You've always got them right on top of you. They're gross. And really dirty. Have you noticed how bad they smell?"

"The eclipse must be starting any second now, right?"

"Have you ever meditated? I've never tried. I can't sit still. I'm very active. I don't think I can sit down without moving around. Without thinking. How can you just stop thinking?" I shrugged my shoulders and raised my eyebrows. I didn't speak; he wasn't waiting for an answer. "I'd like to do yoga, too, but I don't have a mat."

I wondered whether it was a good idea to get into the water in the middle of an eclipse. A sunbath and moonbath at the same time, a day-bath and night-bath. I thought of encounters. And differences. India and Pakistan. You don't often have the chance to live in both night and day, and in the ocean.

"Oh! Osho! Crazy parties! Sexy shit," he said when I described my arrival and short stay with the yogini in her hut. "So little Miss Piggy is gone. Good. She wasn't nice at all."

When the eclipse began, I ran out toward the water, but I stopped on the sand, looking up at the sky with my protective X-ray. It was incredible; I could see it perfectly through the paper. One circle slowly covering up the other. The moon stepping in between the sun and the earth. I think. It really was strange that Erika hadn't mentioned it before she left. I thought about how bizarre it all was. And for some reason, thinking about everything and nothing, it was as if the eclipse exploded and flooded the beach with light, a light that hurt my eyes and made me shield myself, close my eyes furiously, hide. A rock pitched straight into my skull, opened it up, made me understand. Heartbreak hit me with full force, retroactively. I'd read it somewhere, years ago, and it's true. You always know, but sometimes you don't want to know. Free fall. I didn't want to feel the vertigo. I couldn't crash. Not here. Not now, I told myself. I dropped the negative and the sarong. I walked into the water. I felt very good.

I wandered around the rest of the afternoon. I went shopping: I bought a pashmina for Lupe, a Shiva carving for Caboose, a carving of Sita and Rama, a dress. I needed light clothes. I drifted. I went into the internet café. I took a photo of the keyboard and answered Carlos and Lupe. After another dip in the ocean and another walk on the shore, I returned to the hut to shower and change. That night I found my neighbor in the same spot. During the time we hung out, he repeated his name three times and my head stayed in the clouds all three. I didn't understand anything he said, but I didn't ask him anything else, either. Anyway.

We walked along the beach in the direction of the main roads and passed the platform, which was all set up but still empty. We continued toward one of the bars. Thatched roof, wooden chairs and tables, a wooden bar, a sand floor. A blackboard announcing drinks in multicolored chalk: *indian delight, transcendental journey, trance party, palolem dream, illumination power.* I remembered my blue Antarctic cocktail and ordered a shot of tequila and a Foster's Lager. He got a *transcendental journey.* Another shot and another beer, an *indian delight.* He liked the names; he made fun of them, but he had his favorites. To my surprise and relief, he wasn't talking much this time. We sat looking out at the scenery, the people, the night. I suddenly realized he was scouting out two tourist girls and I felt better. He brought them to the bar. They were German. They'd just arrived and they'd missed the eclipse. I was sipping my second Foster when I caught myself thinking about Erika. My neighbor threw back the rest of his drink, got to his feet, and went to dance with one of the girls.

I don't know how I ended up having a conversation about Kurt Cobain and Courtney Love. They were talking about her role in his suicide. How she'd made him so jealous she pushed him to the brink. Apparently she liked to provoke him, enjoyed making him suffer.

"They were Shiva and Shakti," said the other German girl. It was so early and she was already so drunk. "Kurt and Courtney are the same name. They're named the same. Two names for the same being."

"All music's worthless after Nirvana," said one of the guys she was talking with.

"No, my friend. After grunge. It's all worthless after grunge," the other disputed. "Those years weren't marked by Nirvana. It was the whole movement. What about Stone Temple Pilots, what about Pearl Jam?"

"Fuck you! What are you talking about? They totally fall short. Grunge was Nirvana! No, grunge was *Kurt,*" said the first man, standing up and puffing out his chest. "Now we've got all this other shit. Techno, pop ballads, all shit." He raised his voice, brandishing his beer bottle toward the DJ, then slamming it down on the bar so hard I jumped.

I rose from the stool, attempting a smile that no one returned. Maybe no one noticed I was leaving. Not a trace of my neighbor or his new friend. I walked along the beach, uncomfortable. I climbed the stairs, looking down at my dry feet. Tomorrow, a pedicure and a foot massage. When I got to the top, I lifted my eyes and found the door ajar. I took a couple steps backward. I leaned over the balcony and peered toward the sand. I looked through a gap in the palm-leaf wall and couldn't see anyone inside. I called out to the beach for help. I'd left a plastic bottle of mineral water by the door. It had been opened, emptied onto the floor, and crushed into an accordion.

"Hey! Dude!" I shouted to my neighbor—I thought I could hear something next door. Nothing. I knocked on his door. Nothing. I went back. Standing on the sand, I screamed with rage. Panic and rage. Don't let them smell your fear, Bird. They smell it, you're fucked.

"Hey! What's going on here?" I yelled. "Who's there?"

In the eye. You look it in the eye. You look your fear in the eye. I climbed the stairs, slamming my feet into every wooden step. Make noise. They smell your fear and you're fucked. I shouted again, entering the room to turn on the light bulb that hung from the ceiling.

"Hey! What the fuck is going on here?"

Silence.

With the light on and the door still open behind me, I crouched down. I looked under the bed. Heart hammering. My things strewn all over the place. Your eyes can take in five meters of space in two seconds. They'd taken my camera. They'd taken the bags of gifts I'd just bought, scattered everything around the room. The top of my backpack was open. My passport. The little box of candy with no candy in it. The photo of my mother, the crystal. That was it. I went out to the balcony, stumbled down the stairs, ran as fast as I could. I threw up as far away as possible. I splashed seawater on my face, my legs. Goddammit, can't you leave me in peace? I screamed, or roared, or wept, to no one. To the waves.

I ended up curled in a ball on top of the rumpled sheets. I couldn't sleep. I barricaded the door with the mattress. There were sounds coming from the hut next door. *Sail away with me honey, now, now, now...what will be will be.* Or maybe there had been music all along and I was only noticing it now. Was my neighbor with the German girl? What was her name again? I was about to go out and knock again, but I decided he was probably with her. Elsa? It wasn't as if I really liked the guy, anyway. I thought that if I left the light on and the bed against the door, nothing else could happen. What else could possibly happen to you? Jesus fucking Christ. I fell asleep to the faint, fading voice of David Gray singing in my neighbor's hut.

When I woke the next day, I noted that the left-hand corner had gotten wet. My nearly empty pack beside me. The yellow sun outside. The waves breaking. Muffled laughter. *Matter is energy, Energy is Light, We are all light beings.* Albert Einstein.

The first task at hand was to look for a hotel room, try to move. No more huts. Finding nothing available, I stopped at the internet café to check my email and ask them to store my things for a while. I wrote to the couple in Bangalore, not thinking. That was the least I could do, I thought. Thank them. I also thought that teaching tightrope classes was a very bad idea. Too tiring, too hot. The air-conditioning was doing me good. There I was.

As soon as I set foot on the sidewalk, I was burning up again. Pondering whether I should return to the icebox or keep toasting my skin in the sun, I ran into Elsa, one of the German girls. Something strange happened. Our eyes met and she immediately looked away, changed direction, and walked faster, before I could even greet her aloud. I let her go. Who knows what's up with her, I thought. But the bad taste in my mouth instantly returned, the same unease from the night before. Something was off. I walked through the crowds of people, looking for her. Something's not right, I told myself. I focused my attention entirely on searching for her. Palolem isn't that big, I was telling myself, just as I found her at a stall in the market.

"Hey!"

Nothing.

"Hey, you!"

She turned to look at me and vanished again behind one of the countless walls covered in handbags, tank-tops, sarongs.

I decided to drop it. I felt weird about how intensely she was avoiding me. What had I ever done to her? What's wrong with people, dammit? I thought, and then I saw her again, at the front door of a house, trying hurriedly to get inside. When she saw me, she sat down on the ground and burst into tears.

"Get away from me! Where's your friend? Where is that son of a bitch?" she shouted, her face crumpling. She swung her hands at me when I came closer. Motherfucker, she kept saying.

There wasn't much to say.

"He gave me something to drink. Something clear. It wasn't tequila. I don't know what it was. That and two drags on a joint. That was it: one drink and two drags. That was all," she insisted, weeping. "I swear I said no." After a few moments, as I stroked her hair and tried to calm her down—but it was good to cry, I said, she should cry as much as she needed to—she asked, "And you? Why did you move?"

"Because I didn't want to be alone."

"I was shaking all over. I tried to stand up. I was really dizzy and had to sit down. I didn't tell him I wasn't feeling well. I didn't know,

I thought I'd be fine, I swear! But I couldn't even make it down the stairs. Everything was spinning."

The German girl rocked back and forth, pressing her hands into her head, pulling at her own hair. We were a horrible sight.

"I was about to throw up, but he kept offering it to me and I was afraid to say no. But I already made it for you! You're so boring! he said. You're not going to make me throw it away, are you? he said. And he scared me. I didn't want him to get mad."

"You don't have to explain anything to me."

"But I should have screamed! Why didn't I scream? Why didn't I scream?" she asked, looking up at the sky. "He lay me down on his bed. He pulled my skirt up to my waist. He put me face-up and then face-down, and I can't understand why but I couldn't make any decisions at all. He spanked me. I think he laughed. I don't have any condoms! I said. And he laughed, I think. Don't worry, bitch. I'm not going to fuck you, he said. That's what he said."

The German girl was inconsolable. Her face was bright red, her eyes inflamed. She buried her face in her hands almost the entire time. I started to cry, too.

"I was alone when I woke up. I think he left. And I don't think I can report him. I went into his hut because I wanted to, didn't I? And I smoked because I wanted to, right? What would I say to the police?"

"Nothing. Are you sure he left?"

Elsa couldn't stop crying. We went to buy some coconut water. We walked along the beach. The subject emerged and re-emerged between silences. Sharp waves. Curse, hammer, nightmare waves.

"I don't know where the fuck my passport is. I don't know if he stole it or I lost it. And how do I report that?"

"We're not going to report anything."

And again. The incomprehensible movie would resume in her head.

"I don't really remember," she'd say, crying. All that impotence in her tears. "How the fuck is it possible that I can't remember if he fucked me or not?"

The bar staff was getting set up. It was incredible how they could assemble and disassemble a bar in an hour. Every night or every dawn, they'd leave only the rustic wooden bar, the thatched roof. Nothing else. As soon as they'd revive from their nightly plunge off the cliff, the blenders and concoctions would re-materialize. The music would start up again.

"How long are you staying?"

"I don't know. I'm leaving soon."

Elsa stopped short when she saw the group of huts. "Let's go back," she said. She panicked when she realized what I had in mind. "Are you crazy? We have to get out of here."

"I want to give you something before I go."

"Let's go! Please! What if he shows up?" she asked, trembling.

"He's not coming back," I improvised. The door swung open with a single push. The place had things in it. His things.

"He hasn't left! Let's go, please! I'm begging you."

There were two bottles of clear liquor on the table, a couple of glasses, mineral water. Two carved wooden boxes, open and empty. A dictionary. A David Gray CD. I listened to that music for weeks afterward. I sat down on the bed under a mosquito net made from such exotic gauzy cloth that the sight was annoying. The place looked like the backdrop of a theater.

"It looks like the set of *The Beach*!" I exclaimed. "Elsa. Tell me it doesn't look like *The Beach*." Which got a smile out of her. Whenever I'd turn my back, she'd move toward the door again. I found her looking out at the shore, keeping watch.

"Give me a hand with this. Let the door shut and come here. Come on, help me out!"

We lifted up the mattress. I found my camera. It had no case, no lens cap; it was coated in sand. On the floor, in a corner, was the

German girl's passport and hoop earrings. Erika's yoga mat. No money. There was a CD player. A medium-sized ziplock bag of weed. The rumble of the ocean sounded close and aggressive. Voices passed by. They moved slowly. It's tough, walking on sand. I tucked the bag of weed under my bathing suit and sarong.

"What are you doing?" Elsa asked, laughing nervously every few seconds. I took my things. We surveyed the shelf for the last time. In the doorway, about to leave, Elsa came back.

"Let's wrap this up. Hurry! Come on!"

She knocked everything onto the ground, yanked down the tulle canopy, and tried to set fire to the pages of a book with a lighter she found on the bedside table. Things don't burn so easily. It went out right away. She tried again. Nothing. She ripped out a few pages. She pulled down her underpants beneath her dress and peed.

"What the hell are you doing? Let's go! Jesus, we have to go."

Down on the sand, we walked as if everything were perfectly normal, looking straight ahead, walking as fast as we could without calling attention to ourselves. I dropped the bag of weed and snatched it up again. Once we'd put some distance between us and the hut, we broke into a run, laughing wildly, in crisis.

A week later, I saw on the BBC that a nineteen-year-old Australian girl had turned up dead in Palolem. Some fishermen found her at the water's edge. Her photo appeared on the news, her passport photo. She'd been traveling alone for two months and had been at the beach for three days. According to the police, she'd been talking with a drug-dealing tourist and a bartender a few hours before her death. Witnesses saw her leaving the bar with both of them. They'd drugged her and raped her and left her on the beach. I imagined her wet hair, a blonde darkened by all that night, tangled with seaweed and sand. Her skin very red after those last and only days of Indian sun, crisscrossed with lines from her bathing suit, her chest bright white. Her parents had already arrived in town, the news said. They'd identified the body and were preparing to take her home.

I learned that Elsa would travel to London. I'd go to Bangalore by train, my near-empty pack crinkled as a raisin. Federica and Dylan would meet me at the station. My camera survived. It took me several weeks to check the photos, but I finally dared to look at them. I made a selection with the thought of putting together a book. I never heard from Erika. Her hut stayed behind, with a new lock and key, and her quote still on the wall. ☐

Chapter XXIII

I close my eyes to the clatter of the train wheels over the tracks. It's very hot. I find myself lying on my back in a meadow. The ground is wet beneath me, and the part of my clothing that touches the earth is a little colder than the rest. I feel snowflakes melting on my face, on the backs of my hands. I feel the heat. I hear the wheels striking against the iron in the distance. I make my way toward a house. I open a box. I'm holding a letter in my hand and I hear my mother's voice. Everything's always beginning. Think of little kids; they can't measure time. They don't need to. Something ends and something is reborn. We cross the street, hand in hand. Think of animals. We're in a playground paved with gravel. See-saws. I'm in her belly, surrounded by water. An embryo, half sperm, half egg. A cell, an indivisible atom. I'm an invisible dot. I hear something beating. I hear an eternal big bang. I wake to a touch on my shoulder, a voice. We're here, madam. I open my eyes and find a city of gardens outside. I haven't seen them yet, but they announce themselves. I get off the train. White light. I walk out onto the street. I grip my camera. I think it's the end of the animal days. I think the eclipse is over. ⊞

Keila Vall de la Ville is a New York-based Venezuelan author. Her novel *Los días animales* (2016) received the International Latino Book Award for Best Novel 2018. She is the author of the short story collections *Ana no duerme y otros cuentos* (2007), fiction finalist in the Concurso de Cuentos Monte Ávila Editores 2006, and *Enero es el mes más largo* (2021). She has published the poetry collection *Viaje legado* (2016) and edited the bilingual anthology *Between the Breath and the Abyss: Poetics on Beauty* (2021), a compilation of essays and poems by thirty-three contemporary poets on the subject of beauty. Her books *De cuando Corre Lola Corre dejó sin aire a Murakami, and des / encanto* will be published in late 2021. She has a BA in Anthropology (UCV), an MA in Political Science (USB), an MFA in Creative Writing (NYU), and an MA in Hispanic Cultural Studies (Columbia University). She is the mother of two boys and rock-climbing has been part of her life for twenty-five years; she won a silver medal at the Pan-American Climbing Championship in 1996. ✠

Robin Myers is a Mexico City-based poet and translator. Her book-length translations include *The Restless Dead* by Cristina Rivera Garza, *Cars on Fire* by Mónica Ramón Ríos, *Animals at the End of the World* by Gloria Susana Esquivel, *Empty Pool* by Isabel Zapata, and *Lyric Poetry Is Dead* by Ezequiel Zaidenwerg. She was among the winners of the 2019 Poems in Translation Contest (Words Without Borders/Academy of American Poets). Her own poetry collections have been published in Mexico, Argentina, and Spain. 卐

Made in the USA
Columbia, SC
04 September 2021